HEALTH CARE IN TRANSITION

MEDICARE'S PRESCRIPTION DRUG PROGRAM

COMPETITION ISSUES AND COST TRENDS

HEALTH CARE IN TRANSITION

Additional books in this series can be found on Nova's website under the Series tab.

Additional e-books in this series can be found on Nova's website under the e-book tab.

HEALTH CARE IN TRANSITION

MEDICARE'S PRESCRIPTION DRUG PROGRAM

COMPETITION ISSUES AND COST TRENDS

GLORIA R. PATTINSON
EDITOR

nova publishers
New York

For permission to use material from this book please contact us:
Telephone 631-231-7269; Fax 631-231-8175
Web Site: http://www.novapublishers.com

Library of Congress Cataloging-in-Publication Data

ISBN: 978-1-63463-122-8

Published by Nova Science Publishers, Inc. † New York

CONTENTS

PREFACE

This book discusses the cost trends and competition issues of Medicare's Prescription Drug Program.

Chapter 1 - The Medicare Prescription Drug, Improvement, and Modernization Act of 2003 (generally referred to as the Medicare Modernization Act, or MMA) substantially expanded the federal Medicare program by creating the prescription drug benefit known as Part D. In fiscal year 2013, Medicare Part D covered 39 million people. The federal government spent $59 billion net of premiums on Part D in that year; after accounting for certain payments from states under the program, the net federal cost was $50 billion, which represented 10 percent of net federal spending for Medicare. A combination of broader trends in the prescription drug market and lower-than-expected enrollment in Part D has contributed to much lower spending for the program—about 50 percent lower in 2013—than the Congressional Budget Office (CBO) projected when the MMA became law in 2003.

Chapter 2 - Medicare's outpatient prescription drug benefit for senior citizens and people with disabilities, known as Part D, began in 2006. Part D uses private plans to provide coverage for prescription drugs to enrollees. The federal government does not mandate the amounts that plans pay for prescription drugs; instead, plans directly negotiate payment rates with pharmacies and rebates from drug manufacturers while competing with each other for enrollees. Such competition provides incentives for plans to control their costs. One important way in which plans seek to control costs is by encouraging the use of generic drugs. Plans can encourage enrollees to switch from brand-name drugs to their less expensive generic equivalents, a practice known as generic substitution. Plans can also encourage enrollees to switch from a brand-name drug to the generic form of a different drug that is in the same therapeutic class, one form of a practice known as therapeutic substitution. This Congressional Budget Office (CBO) study uses data on Medicare Part D prescription drug insurance claims from the Centers for Medicare and Medicaid Services (CMS) to assess how successful plans have been in encouraging the use of generic drugs and the potential for savings from the additional use of such drugs.

Chapter 3 - The centerpiece of the Medicare Prescription Drug, Improvement, and Modernization Act of 2003 (Medicare Modernization Act) was the creation of Medicare Part D, a subsidized pharmaceutical benefit that went into effect in 2006. That additional coverage—which provides outpatient prescription drug insurance to seniors and to people under age 65 with certain disabilities— constituted the most substantial expansion of the Medicare program since its inception in 1965. In 2010, the federal government spent $62.0 billion on Part D, representing 12 percent of total federal spending for Medicare that year.

Under Medicare Part D, all enrollees receive a subsidy for prescription drug insurance; an additional low-income subsidy (LIS) is available to enrollees with sufficiently low income and assets. (In this issue brief, Part D enrollees who receive the LIS benefit are referred to as LIS enrollees; all others are referred to as non-LIS enrollees.) Enrollees in Part D choose a prescription drug insurance plan from a number of competing private plan sponsors. Total spending on Part D drugs equals the sum of spending by all payers combined, including plan sponsors, beneficiaries, the federal government, and third-party payers; in this brief, it is measured on a per-beneficiary basis. In 2008—the most recent year for which data were available when the Congressional Budget Office (CBO) undertook this analysis—average spending for non-LIS enrollees was $1,800. The amount of spending varied widely across enrollees in that category: for 7 percent, no spending occurred, whereas for 6 percent, the amount was at least $5,000. Enrollees who spent more tended to fill more prescriptions and more-expensive prescriptions. The federal government covered roughly 40 percent of nonLIS spending through premium subsidies, and beneficiaries covered most of the remainder through premium payments and out-of-pocket spending.

Average spending for LIS enrollees in 2008 was $3,600, double the spending for non-LIS enrollees. A slightly larger share of LIS enrollees (9 percent) had no Part D spending, but a much greater share (23 percent) had spending of at least $5,000. As with the non-LIS population, higher spending among LIS enrollees was driven by beneficiaries who filled more prescriptions and who filled more-expensive prescriptions. The higher spending among LIS beneficiaries most likely reflected that group's generally poorer health status and the more generous coverage available through the low-income subsidy. Because of that additional subsidy, the federal government covered 95 percent of LIS spending in 2008.

This issue brief reviews patterns of Medicare Part D utilization and spending among the non-LIS and LIS populations. Other important topics relating to Part D, such as the provision of public benefits by sponsors of private plans and competition among those sponsors, are beyond the scope of this analysis.

In: Medicare's Prescription Drug Program
Editor: Gloria R. Pattinson
ISBN: 978-1-63463-122-8

Chapter 1

COMPETITION AND THE COST OF MEDICARE'S PRESCRIPTION DRUG PROGRAM*

Anna Cook and Andrew Stocking

SUMMARY

The Medicare Prescription Drug, Improvement, and Modernization Act of 2003 (generally referred to as the Medicare Modernization Act, or MMA) substantially expanded the federal Medicare program by creating the prescription drug benefit known as Part D. In fiscal year 2013, Medicare Part D covered 39 million people. The federal government spent $59 billion net of premiums on Part D in that year; after accounting for certain payments from states under the program, the net federal cost was $50 billion, which represented 10 percent of net federal spending for Medicare. A combination of broader trends in the prescription drug market and lower-than-expected enrollment in Part D has contributed to much lower spending for the program—about 50 percent lower in 2013—than the Congressional Budget Office (CBO) projected when the MMA became law in 2003.

* This is an edited, reformatted and augmented version of a report issued by the Congressional Budget Office, July 2014.

Most beneficiaries of Part D choose among private drug plans to receive their coverage; others have employment-based coverage subsidized by Medicare Part D. The competitive design of Part D enables it to adapt flexibly to changing conditions, because plan sponsors (private insurance firms, each of which may offer several different plans) have ongoing incentives to develop new ways to control drug spending so as to minimize their costs, keep premiums low, and attract enrollees. Using the first few years of data from the Part D program, CBO found that spending was lower in years when, and in areas of the country where, more plan sponsors competed for beneficiaries. CBO's analysis suggests that competition between plan sponsors in Part D could be strengthened further, and costs lowered further, through certain changes in the rules of the program, although such changes could have disadvantages as well.

Other government programs use different approaches to deliver prescription drug benefits and hold down the costs of those benefits. In particular, the joint federal-state Medicaid program does not rely on competition between plan sponsors to constrain drug costs; instead, the program's chief cost management tool is statutory rebates that are applied to market-based prices. CBO found that Medicaid pays lower prices than Medicare, on average, for the mix of prescription drugs purchased by Medicare enrollees, primarily because the rebates that the law requires on brand-name drugs under Medicaid are larger than the ones that plan sponsors negotiate with manufacturers under Part D. If policymakers implemented Medicaid's statutory rebates for Part D beneficiaries with low income, but otherwise left Part D unchanged, federal costs would be reduced substantially in the short term. However, firms would respond by charging higher prices before rebates for new drugs (thereby probably offsetting a substantial portion of the savings for the federal government over the longer term) and by curtailing drug innovation.

Why Has the Part D Program Cost Less than Anticipated?

Broad national trends in the prescription drug market have contributed significantly to the lower-than-expected spending for Part D. Many health care analysts, including those at CBO, expected in 2003 that growth in national drug spending would slow from the rapid rates observed in the late 1990s and early 2000s, but the magnitude of the slowdown that occurred surprised many observers. Drug spending per person for the country as a whole increased by only 2 percent per year, on average, between 2007 and 2010, compared with average growth of 13 percent per year between 1999 and 2003, the five-year period before enactment of the MMA. Drug spending per person in Part D also increased by 2 percent per year, on average, between 2007 and 2010. The greater-than-expected slowdown that began after 2003 caused national drug spending in 2012 to be about 40 percent less than the amount predicted by analysts at the Centers for Medicare & Medicaid Services in 2003.

Two developments accounted for much of the slowdown in growth of national drug spending per person:

- Many existing brand-name drugs lost their patent protection and faced new competition from generic substitutes, which have the same active ingredients as their brand-name counterparts but are much less expensive. Between 2007 and 2010, the share of prescriptions filled with generic drugs increased from 67 percent to 78 percent nationwide (and from 63 percent to 73 percent in Part D).
- New brand-name drugs (which tend to be more expensive than older brand-name therapies) were introduced at a slower rate than in the late 1990s.

Spending per beneficiary in Part D has been lower than CBO projected in part because of those developments affecting nationwide drug spending.

In addition to spending per beneficiary, enrollment in Part D has been smaller than CBO initially projected—by about 12 percent in 2012. CBO initially projected the share of eligible people who would enroll in Part D on the basis of enrollment in similar government health care programs—in particular, Part B of Medicare, which is a voluntary program that primarily covers physicians'' and outpatient services for the same population that is eligible for Part D. CBO adjusted that share down-ward slightly to account for potential enrollees who would have prescription drug coverage through another source, among other factors. But the share of Medicare beneficiaries enrolling in Part D has been substantially lower. One contributing factor is probably that beneficiaries need to make an active effort to enroll in Part D—unlike Part B, in which beneficiaries are usually enrolled by default and must take steps to opt out.

Taken together, the unexpected slowdown in national drug spending per person and smaller-than-expected enrollment in Part D can account for nearly all of the difference between CBO's original estimate and actual Part D spending. CBO's original estimate incorporated an expectation that elements of the program's design that were intended to foster price competition between private plans would help to limit costs per beneficiary. Because other factors have affected costs per beneficiary, deter-mining whether the competitive design of the program has been more or less effective than CBO originally anticipated is not feasible.

How Has Competition between Plan Sponsors Affected Part D Spending?

Medicare Part D was designed to foster competition between plan sponsors to constrain drug spending. In assessing the impact of competition, CBO found that a larger number of plan sponsors in a region was associated with lower bids, on average, for the group of plans analyzed.

Each summer, every Part D plan submits a bid that reflects the total amount it would be willing to accept to offer Part D coverage for a Medicare beneficiary of aver-age health for the following year. Once the bids from all plans have been submitted, the government determines the amount it will pay toward the benefit for the average beneficiary. The premium for each plan depends on the difference between a plan's bid and the government's payment. Plans with lower costs can submit lower bids and thus offer lower premiums and attract more beneficiaries. Other features of a plan, such as its cost-sharing provisions and the specific drugs it covers, also influence a plan's attractiveness to potential enrollees.

CBO analyzed bids for "basic stand-alone" Part D plans between 2006 and 2010 and found that plans in regions with more plan sponsors tended to have lower bids and premiums than those in regions with fewer sponsors. (Basic stand-alone Part D plans, which accounted for about half of total Part D enrollment over that period, offer a standard level of prescription drug coverage; CBO excluded from its analysis of plan bids stand-alone plans that offer more generous drug benefits, employment-based plans, and plans that combine drug coverage with coverage for other medical benefits, such as hospitalization and physicians' services.) Between 2006 and 2007, an average of 6 new plan sponsors joined the market in each of the 34 Part D regions that together cover the United States, contributing to lower bids and lower government spending. However, between 2007 and 2010, the average total number of plan sponsors per region fell by 4 (from 22 to 18), because more sponsors exited the market or merged with other sponsors than entered the market; that decrease in competition is associated with higher bids and higher government spending.

As Part D is currently structured, two features of the program could be changed to encourage plan sponsors to submit lower bids for their plans. First, in the component of Part D that serves low-income beneficiaries, the government usually pays the full amount of a plan's bid up to a threshold, regardless of whether other plans bid lower. Second, low-income beneficiaries enrolled in plans whose bid rises above the threshold are automatically reassigned in equal proportions to plans with bids below the threshold (unless a beneficiary has *actively* signed up for a particular plan). Both of those features encourage plans to set their bids close to (though below) the threshold.

Has Growth in Payments to Part D Plans been in Line with Growth in Drug Spending?

The payments to plans by the government and beneficiaries for the basic Part D benefit increased more rapidly between 2007 and 2010 than did spending for drugs by those plans. Specifically, the payments to stand-alone plans for the basic benefit grew by 3.3 percent per year per beneficiary, on average, whereas plans' spending per beneficiary on drugs for the basic benefit grew by an average of 2.8 percent per year.

The difference between those growth rates represents an increase in the sum of plans' administrative costs and profits over the 2007–2010 period. Drawing firm conclusions about the cause of that increase is difficult, in part because of the short time frame of the analysis and a lack of information about whether the initial amounts of administrative costs and profits were unusually low. Nonetheless, some increase in the sum of administrative costs and profits could be explained by the reduction in the number of plan sponsors between 2007 and 2010.

How Do Prices for Drugs Differ between Part D and Medicaid?

For the drug classes representing the great majority of drug spending by Part D beneficiaries, CBO found that Medicaid's average price for drugs was between 27 per-cent and 38 percent lower than Part D's average price in 2010 after controlling for differences in health conditions between beneficiaries of the programs. (Prices are measured net of rebates.) CBO expects that the difference in average prices will narrow over time as drug manufacturers respond to new rules that increased Medicaid's rebates beginning in 2010 but that Medicaid's average price will remain at least 20 percent to 30 percent lower than Part D's average price after controlling for differences in health conditions.

The difference in average drug prices between Part D and Medicaid in 2010 occurred primarily because Medicaid's statutory rebates on brand-name drugs were generally much larger than the rebates on those drugs negotiated by plan sponsors in Part D.

Rates of generic drug use were similar in the two programs, so the higher prices paid by Part D for brand-name drugs were not offset by significantly greater use of generic drugs. However, the higher prices for given brand-name drugs were offset in part by greater use in Part D of lower-priced drugs within therapeutic classes (groups of drugs that are intended to treat common sets of medical conditions and that typically have similar modes of action). If the different patterns of use within therapeutic classes stemmed entirely from differences in the structure of the programs, then the lower end of those ranges—27 percent in 2010 and at least 20 percent in the future—reflects the relative effectiveness of those program structures in containing drug prices. If, instead, the different patterns of use within therapeutic classes stemmed entirely from differences in health conditions between beneficiaries of the programs, then the higher end of those ranges—38 percent in 2010 and at least 30 percent in the future— reflects the relative effectiveness of those program structures in containing drug prices.

Some policymakers have proposed applying Medicaid's statutory rebates to drug purchases made by Part D beneficiaries who receive low-income subsidies (while retaining the existing structure of Part D in other respects). CBO expects that adopting such a policy would lower the average cost of brand-name drugs in Part D and thus reduce the federal government's costs over the first decade after the policy was adopted. But a substantial portion of those savings would probably erode over time because drug manufacturers would counter the larger rebates by raising the prices for new brand-name drugs. In addition, that policy would reduce the incentive for firms to develop new drugs.

SECTION 1. THE FEDERAL BUDGETARY COST OF MEDICARE PART D

In 2003, the Congressional Budget Office (CBO) projected that net federal spending for the Medicare Part D program would be $99 billion in fiscal year 2013; actual spending was $50 billion, or nearly 50 percent less than anticipated.[1] Over the 2006–2013 period covered by CBO's original cost estimate, net federal spending for Part D was projected to be $550 billion; actual spending was $353 billion, or 36 percent less.

This section examines the two main factors that primarily account for the lower-than-expected costs.[2] First, the slowdown in nationwide drug spending has been faster than anticipated. CBO estimated in 2003 that the rate of growth in drug spending per person for the nation as a whole would decline gradually toward its average of previous decades but would remain above that average for most of the 10-year projection period (through 2013), consistent with the views of many health care analysts at the time.[3] However, the growth rate of national drug spending per person dropped below its long-term average even before the Part D program was implemented, and the rate has remained low. Because of that lower growth rate, drug spending nationwide in 2012 was about 40 percent less than had been expected by analysts at the Centers for Medicare & Medicaid Services (CMS) in 2003. That difference explains a large share of the amount by which CBO overestimated Part D drug spending for 2012.[4]

Second, participation in Part D has been lower than originally projected. Although CBO estimated that the share of Medicare enrollees who would participate in Part D would be about 7 percent lower than enrollment in Medicare Part B—which turned out to be 92 percent of the total Medicare population in 2012—the actual share of Medicare enrollees in Part D was 21 percent lower, or only 73 percent in 2012. Part B and Part D are similar in several respects, but eligible Medicare beneficiaries are not automatically enrolled in Part D, as they usually are in Part B; instead, they must actively sign up for drug coverage. That requirement may have held down Part D enrollment more than CBO anticipated. In addition, enrollees in Part D are required to choose among various drug plans, whereas enrollees in Part B are not required to make any further choices when enrolling; that difference also may have held down Part D enrollment in a way that CBO did not anticipate. Yet another factor that may have held down Part D enrollment is that Part D covers a smaller share of total medical costs than Part B, on average, and so is less valuable to potential beneficiaries. Partly offsetting its overestimate of the rate of participation in Part D, CBO underestimated the total number of enrollees in Medicare. All told, actual enrollment in Part D in 2012 was about 12 percent lower than CBO expected. That difference in enrollment probably accounts for less than a 12 percent difference in the program's estimated costs, however, because people who have low drug spending are less likely to enroll.

Taken together, the faster-than-expected slowdown in national drug spending per person and the smaller-than-expected enrollment in Part D account for nearly all of the difference between CBO's initial projection and actual Part D spending. CBO's original projection reflected the agency's judgment that elements of the program's design that were intended to foster price competition between private plans would help to limit the costs of Part D, yielding lower costs per enrollee than would be expected for a similar population under a typical employment-based drug plan offered at that time. However, determining whether the actual effects of competition have been larger or smaller than those incorporated in the original estimate is not feasible because many other factors have also affected Part D costs.

Prescription Drug Spending per Person Nationwide and in Medicare Part D

Between 2007 and 2010, per capita drug spending nationwide (reflecting both the net price of drugs and the quantity used) increased by about 2 percent per year, on average. That rate is much lower than the average growth rate of such spending—about 13 percent per year— between 1999 and 2003, the five years before enactment of the Medicare Modernization Act (MMA), the law that created Medicare Part D (see Figure 1-1). The national slowdown in per capita drug spending can largely be attributed to a slowdown in the growth of average prices for drugs, which rose by 9 percent per year nationwide between 1999 and 2003, CBO estimates, but increased much more slowly between 2007 and 2010.[5]

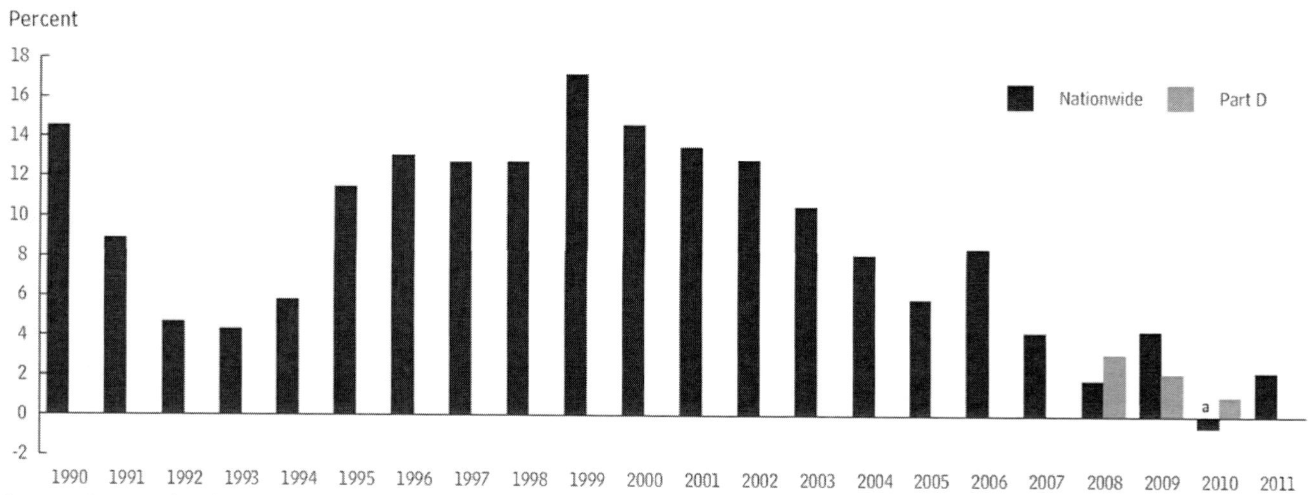

Source: Congressional Budget Office based on the historical national health expenditure accounts and Part D claims and rebate data obtained from the Centers for Medicare & Medicaid Services.

Note: Both nationwide and Part D drug spending are net of rebates. The growth rate of Part D spending in 2007 relative to 2006 is not included because many enrollees did not have coverage for the full year in 2006.

a. The Affordable Care Act (ACA) significantly reduced the prices the federal government pays for prescription drugs under Medicaid beginning in 2010. Medicaid accounted for about 8 percent of total spending in the retail pharmacy market in 2010. Nationwide, drug spending per person fell by 0.4 percent in 2010; without the ACA's reduction in Medicaid's payment rates, the growth rate per person would have been higher by about 0.5 percentage points, yielding growth of drug spending per person of 0.1 percent.

Figure 1-1. Annual Growth Rates of Drug Spending per Person, 1990 to 2011.

Although health care analysts expected a slowdown in per capita spending nationwide because of ongoing changes in the prescription drug market that were independent of the implementation of Part D, spending slowed much more dramatically than most analysts had anticipated. For example, in 2004, CMS projected that drug spending for the nation as a whole would total just over $3 trillion for the 2006–2013 period. By 2006, after enactment of the MMA but before its implementation could have had significant effects, that figure had been revised downward substantially, to $2.3 trillion; the most recent data and projections by CMS suggest that actual spending over the period will be about $2 trillion, or one-third less than CMS had projected around the time that the legislation was enacted.[6] By 2012, drug spending nationwide was about 40 percent less than what CMS had projected for that year in 2003, before enactment of the MMA. Because CBO's expectations for national drug spending were similar to CMS's projections, CBO's original cost estimate for Part D also reflected much higher amounts of drug spending than have occurred.

Two developments in particular contributed to the slow rate of growth in national drug spending after 2003:

- *Patent Expiration and Generic Entry.* Many existing brand-name drugs lost their patent protection, which led to an increase in the introduction and use of less expensive generic substitutes.
- *Slow Entry of New Brand-Name Drugs.* The introduction of new brand-name drugs, which tend to be more expensive than older brand-name therapies, slowed relative to its pace in the late 1990s.

Those developments held down growth in spending per person in Part D as well as nationwide. Between 2007 and 2010, per capita spending on prescription drugs both nationwide and in Part D grew by about 2 percent per year, on average (see Figure 1-1).[7]

To assess the importance of those developments for Part D spending, CBO used data on the claims of Part D beneficiaries and on rebates received between 2007 and 2010 to calculate the changes in the prices (net of rebates) for, and the use of, brand-name and generic drugs. (Comparable data are not readily available for drug spending nationwide.) Between 2007 and 2010, the average price of a 30-day supply of *brand-name* drugs used by Part D beneficiaries rose from $109 to $141, and the average price of a 30-day supply of *generic* drugs fell from $22 to $21 (see Figure 1-2).[8] The expiration of patents on existing brand-name drugs, combined with a slow rate of entry of new brand-name drugs into the market, caused the use of generic drugs as a share of total drugs taken by Part D beneficiaries to increase from 63 percent in 2007 to 73 percent by 2010. Taking those factors together, the average price of a 30-day supply of drugs for Part D beneficiaries fell by less than $1, equaling approximately $54 in both 2007 and 2010. In percentage terms, that decline in the average price was 0.5 percent per year between 2007 and 2010 (see Table 1-1). Over that same period, the average quantity of drugs consumed by Part D beneficiaries rose 2.6 per-cent per year, resulting in an average annual increase of 2.1 percent in drug spending per person.

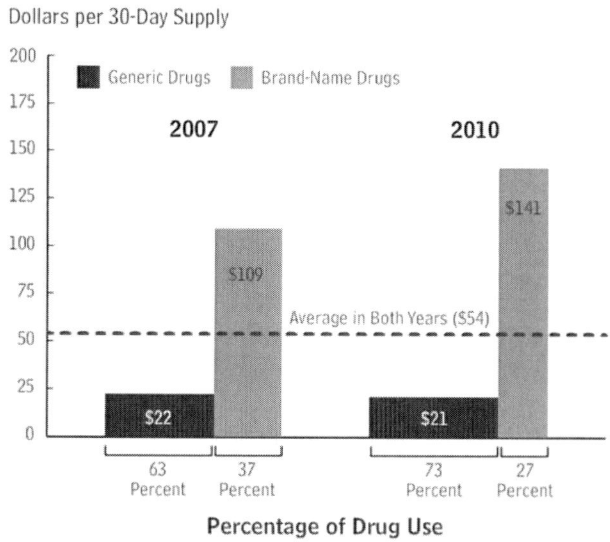

Source: Congressional Budget Office based on Medicare Part D claims data and summary data on total manufacturer rebates paid to Part D plans (obtained from the Centers for Medicare & Medicaid Services), as well as *Red Book* data (available from Truven Health Analytics) to determine whether a drug was brand-name or generic.

Note: Prices for brand-name drugs are net of rebates.

Figure 1-2. Changes in the Use of and Prices for Brand-Name and Generic Drugs in Medicare Part D between 2007 and 2010.

Table 1-1. Average Drug Prices, Quantities, and Spending under Part D, 2007 to 2010

	2007	2008	2009	2010	Average Increase per Year (Percent)
Price of a 30-Day Supply[a] (Dollars)	54.3	53.8	53.7	53.5	-0.5
Quantity of Drugs Consumed (Number of 30-day supplies per person)	42.5	44.1	45.2	45.9	2.6
Drug Spending[b] (Dollars per person)	2,304	2,376	2,428	2,453	2.1
Memorandum:					
Rebates as a Share of Total Retail Spending (Percent)	9.7	10.4	11.1	11.3	5.3
Generic Drugs as a Share of the Number of 30-Day Supplies (Percent)	63	68	70	73	5.0

Source: Congressional Budget Office based on Medicare Part D claims data and summary data on total manufacturer rebates paid to Part D plans (obtained from the Centers for Medicare & Medicaid Services), as well as *Red Book* data (available from Truven Health Analytics) to determine whether a drug was brand-name or generic.

a. The price of a 30-day supply represents the average price of brand-name and generic drugs, net of rebates.

b. Spending per person equals the price of a 30-day supply multiplied by the number of 30-day supplies per person.

Patent Expiration and Generic Entry

From 2007 to 2010, many brand-name drugs lost their patent protection and faced new competition from generic substitutes. Those developments contributed to an increase in the share of prescriptions nationwide for which a generic version is available from 74 percent in 2007 to 84 percent in 2010; within Part D, the increase was similar. Over the same period, the use of generic drugs nationwide as a share of all drugs rose from 67 percent to 78 percent—an increase roughly equivalent to that observed in the Part D market.

The increased use of generic drugs stems from two types of substitution, both of which reduced the average price of drugs used. First, generic drugs were substituted for their brand-name counterparts that lost patent protection. Such substitution decisions are guided by state laws and often made by the pharmacist or the beneficiary (a decision based partly on the drug's relative copayment, or the amount the beneficiary pays to fill the prescription) and typically do not require permission from the pre-scribing physician. Between 2007 and 2010, more than 90 percent of prescriptions were filled with a generic alternative (when one was available) within 12 months of patent expiration; that share was larger than was observed in 2002, for example, when 72 percent of prescriptions were filled with an available generic alternative within 12 months of patent expiration.[9]

Second, physicians shifted away from treatments with only brand-name drugs to treatments with different active ingredients that are therapeutically similar (in other words, that use similar means for controlling a symptom or condition and have comparable effects) but that exist in generic form. For example, many brand-name "statin" drugs were available to treat high cholesterol in that period, with some available in generic form and others not. Only the prescribing physician, not the beneficiary or pharmacist, can determine whether such substitutions to therapeutically similar drugs are appropriate. Although both types of substitution appear to be occurring, CBO has not quantified the contribution of each type to the total shift to generic drugs.[10]

Spending data available for Part D beneficiaries illustrate the extent to which generic entry can reduce the average retail price of drugs (see Table 1-2). (The retail price is the price paid by Part D plans to retail pharmacies for drugs purchased by beneficiaries and is higher than the net price, which includes the rebates that Part D plan sponsors negotiate with manufacturers.) For brand-name drugs that remained protected by patents, the average retail price increased by 8.5 percent annually, on average, between 2007 and 2010. By contrast, the weighted average retail price of brand-name drugs that had recently lost patent protection and of their generic counterparts decreased by 19.8 percent annually, on average, over that period.[11] And the weighted average retail price of drugs that were already available in both brand-name and generic versions fell by 3.4 percent annually, on average, during those years. Hypothetically, if none of the patent expirations since 2006 had occurred, so that none of those drugs had faced new competition from generic drugs (and there were no other differences in the drug market), the average retail price of a 30-day supply of drugs in Part D would have increased by about 5 percent annually, on average—much faster than the observed average increase of 1.2 percent per year.[12]

The increased use of generic drugs has generate substantial savings in Part D. CBO estimated that the use of generic drugs instead of their brand-name counterparts saved $33 billion in 2007, reducing total spending on prescription drugs within the program from $93 billion (if no generic drugs had been available) to $60 billion.[13]

Slow Entry of New Brand-Name Drugs

The Food and Drug Administration approved about 40 percent fewer new brand-name drugs each year, on average, between 2007 and 2010 than in the late 1990s. Between 1996 and 1999, 39 brand-name drugs representing new chemical entities were approved each year, on average; between 2007 and 2010, that figure was just 22, on average (although it jumped up to 39 in 2012 before receding to 27 in 2013).[14]

Table 1-2. Changes in Average Retail Drug Prices in Part D, 2007 to 2010

Percent				
Drug Product Group[a]	**2007 to 2008**	**2008 to 2009**	**2009 to 2010**	**Percent Average Change per Year**
Patent-Protected Brand-Name Drugs	7.8	9.0	8.7	**8.5**
Recently Off-Patent Brand-Name Drugs and Generic Counterparts[b]	-19.7	-21.5	-18.0	**-19.8**
Older Off-Patent Brand-Name Drugs and Generic Counterparts	-3.5	-2.2	-4.7	**-3.4**
All Drugs	0.4	2.0	1.2	**1.2**

Source: Congressional Budget Office based on Medicare Part D claims data (obtained from the Centers for Medicare & Medicaid Services) and *Red Book* data (available from Truven Health Analytics) to determine whether a drug was brand-name or generic.

Note: The change in prices is based on the set of drugs purchased in the initial year of the time period analyzed. The average price for a drug product group is calculated by weighting the price of a particular product in the group by the number of days for which that product was supplied. "Drug products" combine brand-name products with their generic counterparts having the same chemical entity, dosage form, and strength. (Over time, as new generic drugs are substituted for their higher-priced brand-name counterparts, the average price of a drug product generally declines.)

a. The drugs included in each product group change somewhat over time. That change can occur, for example, when a brand-name drug loses its patent protection and moves to recently off-patent status.

b. Recently off-patent brand-name drugs include drugs that first experienced competition from generic drugs in the year prior to the period analyzed through the end of the period analyzed. For example, for the 2007–2008 period, that category includes drugs that first experienced generic competition between 2006 and 2008, and for the 2009–2010 period, it includes drugs that first experienced generic competition between 2008 and 2010.

Certain new drugs tend to increase in price and quantity sold as they become more widely recognized; thus, total spending climbs rapidly for new drugs that become top sellers over the first several years they are on the market.[15] The introduction of many new drugs in the late 1990s contributed to higher rates of growth in drug spending in the early 2000s. By contrast, fewer new drugs were launched in the United States per year over the 2004– 2010 period (especially in 2007 and 2008), which contributed to declining spending on new drugs from 2007 to 2010.[16] Indeed, all of the top 20 drugs in 2010, as measured by sales, had been introduced by 2004.

In particular, a smaller number of brand-name drugs reached "blockbuster" status (more than $1 billion in annual sales nationwide) between 2007 and 2010 than earlier in the decade. Although the total number of blockbuster drugs increased each year between 1997 and 2006, it declined between 2007 and 2010 because of patent expirations, causing the average prices for a number of drugs to fall.[17] The emergence of fewer blockbuster drugs may also have constrained growth in the quantity of drugs consumed; that quantity can increase if new blockbuster drugs represent previously unavailable treatments or allow beneficiaries to substitute a drug therapy for a medical procedure.[18]

The smaller number of new blockbuster drugs since 2007 stems in part from a decrease in the rate of introduction of drugs that treat diseases or conditions affecting many people.[19] New brand-name drugs are categorized in one of three ways: as a novel treatment (the first product with approval from the Food and Drug Administration to use a certain mechanism to treat a particular disease), as a new drug that extends an existing treatment mechanism, or as an orphan drug (one that treats rare diseases affecting fewer than 200,000 people). The number of novel treatments per year fell from an average of 14 in 2002 and 2003 to an average of 7 between 2007 and 2010. In contrast, the introduction of drugs that extended existing treatment mechanisms rose slightly, from an average of 7 to an average of 9 per year, between the 2002–2003 and 2007–2010 periods, and the number of new brand-name drugs classified as orphans increased from an average of 4 to an average of 7 per year over those two time periods.[20]

The reduced introduction of novel treatments and the relatively constant introduction of drugs that extended existing treatment mechanisms, combined with patent expirations, contributed to a decline in the share of prescriptions written for brand-name drugs between 2006 and 2010. Although the slow rate of introduction of new brand-name drugs through 2010, especially drugs reaching blockbuster status, has held down growth in drug spending in recent years, it has also meant that patients have not benefited from new treatments at the same rates as before.

Enrollment in Medicare Part D

Spending in Medicare Part D has also turned out to be lower than CBO originally estimated because enrollment in the program has been lower than the agency expected. CBO based its original estimates largely on historical rates of participation in Medicare Part B, which covers mainly physicians' and outpatient services.[21] Parts B and D of Medicare have several similarities: Both are voluntary programs, provide premium subsidies of about 75 percent, and impose significant penalties for late enrollment. Although 94 percent of Medicare beneficiaries in the early 2000s were enrolled in Part B, CBO estimated that participation in Part D would be slightly lower—about 87 percent—because some Part B enrollees (in particular, federal retirees and some active private-sector workers) would have drug coverage through other sources and therefore would not sign up for Part D. (Retirees from private firms who receive drug coverage through their former employer that is subsidized by Medicare Part D were included in CBO's estimate of Part D participation and are likewise included in counts of Part D enrollees.)

Actual enrollment in Part D in 2012 was 12 percent lower than CBO originally estimated—but because beneficiaries with low drug spending are less likely to enroll in Part D, that difference in enrollment probably accounts for less than a 12 percent difference in the program's costs.[22] Although CBO underestimated the total number of enrollees in Medicare, it overestimated the share of those enrollees who would participate in Part D. In 2012, 73 percent of the total Medicare population enrolled in Part D, which is substantially lower than Part B enrollment (92 percent of Medicare beneficiaries in that year) and also lower than the 87 percent of Medicare beneficiaries CBO originally estimated would enroll in Part D.

One likely reason for the difference in enrollment between Part B and Part D is the default enrollment procedures. Such procedures have been shown in recent studies to significantly affect enrollment rates in various sorts of activities.[23] Most people enroll in Social Security by the time they turn 65; at that point, they are automatically enrolled in Medicare Part A and must take active steps to avoid being enrolled in Part B.[24] By contrast, they are not generally enrolled by default in Part D. That difference may have mattered more than CBO had anticipated.

Another possible reason for lower enrollment in Part D than in Part B is the complexity of the choices involved in signing up for the coverage. When deciding whether to enroll in Part D, Medicare beneficiaries must choose among the various drug plans available to them. For Part B, in contrast, beneficiaries face the much simpler choice of whether or not to enroll in the program. Some researchers have found that giving people an abundance of choices increases the probability that they will make no choice at all, although other researchers have reached the opposite conclusion; CBO's original estimate did not account for a possible effect of that sort.[25]

A third possible reason for lower enrollment in Part D than in Part B is that some Medicare beneficiaries may not value Part D coverage as highly as they value coverage from Part B, which covers a larger share of total medical costs, on average. Again, that factor may have mattered more than CBO had expected.

SECTION 2. THE COMPETITIVE DESIGN OF MEDICARE PART D

Many elements of the Medicare Part D program were designed to foster competition between plan sponsors. When potential enrollees choose between drug plans, they consider various characteristics of those plans, including premiums, the drugs that are covered, the ease of using a plan's network of pharmacies, and other features. Because of the competitive design of Part D, plan sponsors have ongoing incentives to provide a combination of characteristics that attract potential enrollees while keeping premiums low. To keep premiums low, plan sponsors need to hold down costs (see Appendix A for an illustration of how plans' bids are used to deter-mine enrollees' premiums).[26] In the Part D program, plans' premiums and enrollees' choices of plans help determine the costs borne by the federal government, because the government's payments for the basic benefit are based largely on the enrollment-weighted average of plans' bids.

This section examines the ways in which competition between plan sponsors reduces the cost of the Part D program. Using data for the subset of Part D beneficiaries in basic stand-alone plans from the first few years of the Part D program, the Congressional Budget Office found that plans' bids were lower when a larger number of plan sponsors competed in a region.[27] This analysis excludes bids from Medicare Advantage drug plans: Because those plans are offered only in conjunction with coverage for physicians' and hospital services, they present a different set of choices for beneficiaries.[28] (See Box 2-1 for more details about the basic drug benefit.) Between 2006 and 2007, the average number of competing plan sponsors per region increased and bids fell. CBO's analysis implies that bids fell partly because of increased competition and partly for other reasons, including plans' overestimating costs in the first year of the program, when they had no historical experience on which to draw. From 2007 to 2010, by contrast, the average number of competitors per region fell and bids increased somewhat more quickly, on average, than drug spending. Bids increased more in areas with a larger reduction in the number of competitors, which suggests that the sum of profits and administrative costs probably rose more for firms in those areas than for firms in other areas.

Certain rules of the Part D program reduce the incentives for plans to offer lower bids and premiums. Primarily, those rules govern beneficiaries who receive low-income subsidies under Part D, which are substantially greater than the subsidies that other beneficiaries receive. (In general, recipients must have both low income and few assets or resources to qualify for Part D's low-income subsidies, but for simplicity those recipients are referred to as low-income beneficiaries throughout this report.) CBO's analysis suggests that changing the rules to strengthen the incentives for plans to lower their bids could reduce the cost of the program, although those changes could have disadvantages as well.

Box 2-1. The Structure of the Basic Benefit and Federal Payments for Medicare Part D

Two broad categories of plans participate in Medicare Part D: stand-alone prescription drug plans, which enroll beneficiaries who receive their other Medicare coverage through the traditional fee-for-service program, and Medicare Advantage prescription drug plans. (A small share of beneficiaries are enrolled in Part D plans offered through their former employer or union; the Part D program also provides subsidies to retirees who are enrolled in a private employer's or union's plan rather than a Part D plan.) Under Medicare Advantage, enrollees choose among avail-able private health plans for their nondrug Medicare benefits; those enrollees must obtain both prescription drug coverage and nondrug coverage from the same plan, which causes the plans' sponsors to compete for beneficiaries on the basis of the cost and design of their entire insurance product and not just Part D coverage.

For stand-alone and Medicare Advantage plans in 2014, the basic drug benefit has the following standard features:

- No coverage for the first $310 of drug spending (the deductible);
- Coverage for 75 percent of spending between the deductible and an initial coverage limit of $2,850;
- Limited coverage for generic and brand-name drugs when spending is between the initial cover age limit and a catastrophic limit on out-of-pocket costs of $4,550 (a range of spending sometimes referred to as the coverage gap or "doughnut hole"); and
- Coverage for 95 percent of spending above the catastrophic limit.

Basic plans may strictly follow that benefit structure, or they may adjust certain cost-sharing features while covering the same share of drug spending for beneficiaries, on average, as the benefit outlined above—in other words, they may offer a benefit that is "actuarially equivalent," subject to some constraints. In addition to the basic benefit, some plans offer supplemental coverage for which beneficiaries pay an additional premium. Those plans are sometimes referred to as enhanced plans. Benefits offered by enhanced plans may include additional coverage in the coverage gap, lower copayments or coinsurance, or a lower deductible.

Over the 2007–2010 period, almost 80 percent of beneficiaries in stand-alone plans were enrolled in a basic plan, with the remaining share enrolled in enhanced plans. Of the group of beneficiaries in stand-alone plans who were not receiving low-income subsidies, 60 percent were in basic plans and the rest were in enhanced plans.

Under current law, the coverage gap will be phased out by 2020. Since 2011, drug manufacturers have been required to offer a discount of 50 percent on purchases of brand-name drugs in the coverage gap for all beneficiaries who do not have sufficiently low income to qualify for cost-sharing subsidies. In addition, Part D plans will gradually cover a larger share of spending for those beneficiaries each year; by 2020, beneficiaries will be responsible for 25 per-cent of the cost for both brand-name and generic drugs between the deductible and the catastrophic limit. (Beneficiaries receiving low-income subsidies do not face a coverage gap because their cost-sharing subsidies cover most of their out-of-pocket costs.)

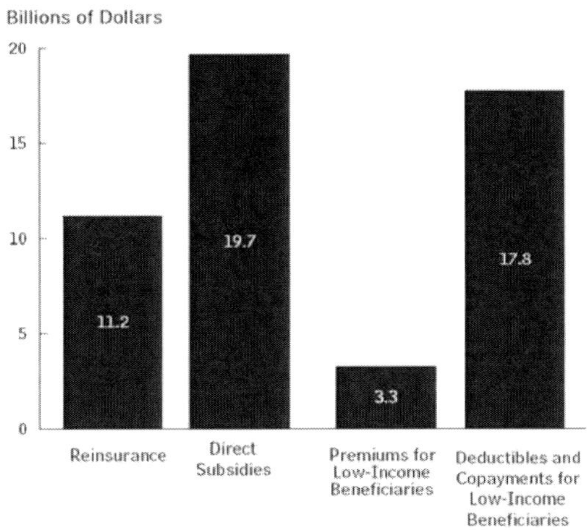

Source: Congressional Budget Office based on data from the Centers for Medicare & Medicaid Services (CMS).

Note: Plan payments are on an incurred basis and exclude risk corridor payments, which are payments made to (or from) the federal government when plans overestimate (or underestimate) their spending relative to actual spending beyond a threshold amount. On net, plans made $0.9billion in risk corridor payments to CMS in 2010.

The Federal Government's Payments to Part D Plans, 2010.

Payments by Part D to each plan reflect the plan's estimated and actual costs, including administrative costs and profits, of providing the basic Part D benefit to an average Medicare beneficiary. Specifically, federal payments to plans for the basic benefit take two forms. First, reinsurance payments cover 80percent of incurred drug costs above the catastrophic limit. Second, direct subsidy payments are based on each plan's bid, which reflects its estimated cost of providing the basic benefit excluding expected reinsurance payments. (For a visual presentation of the calculation of payments to plans by different sources, see Appendix A on page 37.) Together, those two federal payments are designed to equal about 75percent of the average cost of the basic benefit. In 2010, direct subsidy payments totaled $19.7 billion, and reinsurance payments totaled $11.2 billion (see the figure).

The federal government provides additional subsidies for beneficiaries who have income and assets below a certain threshold, many of whom are eligible for both Medicare and Medicaid. People who are eligible for both programs receive a full subsidy to cover their premium—up to a certain limit that is set regionally—plus subsidies to cover most of their deductibles and copayments. Other Medicare beneficiaries with low income and few assets also qualify for additional federal assistance, which ranges from partial to full coverage of their premiums, deductibles, and copayments. In 2010, the additional premium subsidies for low-income beneficiaries totaled $3.3 billion, and subsidies for deductibles and copayments for low-income beneficiaries totaled $17.8 billion. Beneficiaries who do not quality for low-income subsidies generally pay about 25 percent of the average cost of the basic benefit through their premiums. (Beneficiaries with income that exceeds a certain amount are required to pay more than 25 percent of the average cost of the basic benefit.) In addition, they pay any deductible and copayments associated with their plan. As part of those copayments, beneficiaries directly cover 5 percent of spending in excess of the catastrophic limit, and the federal government covers 80 percent of those costs through the reinsurance payments; the expected cost of the remaining 15percent is incorporated into plans' bids.

Beneficiaries' Choices

The main mechanism through which competition in the Medicare Part D market reduces the program's costs has two related components.

First, when beneficiaries select a plan, they tend to select less-expensive plans from among those offered, which provides an incentive for plans to submit low bids. Before the start of each year, beneficiaries are presented with a choice of plans and their associated premiums. Each plan must offer at least the basic level of prescription drug coverage, which makes the plans easier to compare. Although the total cost to a beneficiary includes the premium, deductible, and other out-of-pocket expenses, beneficiaries tend to choose plans with lower premiums, which encourages plans to compete on that basis.[29]

In particular, enrollees tend to choose plans with premiums close to the lower end of the range that is offered. In 2007, the average monthly premium offered across the 34 Part D bidding regions (including both basic and enhanced plans) was about $36. The difference in premiums between the least expensive and most expensive plan exceeded $62 in all regions. (When limited to basic plans only, the difference in premiums between the least expensive and most expensive plan always exceeded $30.) Fifty-five percent of enrollees not receiving a low-income subsidy chose a plan whose premium was within $15 of the least expensive plan in their region, and 75 percent chose a plan whose premium was within $20 of the least expensive plan in their region.[30]

Second, plans have a significant number of potential new enrollees each year, which encourages competition between plan sponsors. At the end of each year, there is an open-enrollment period for the coming year. In general, plans can change their benefits and premiums only at that time, and most beneficiaries can choose a plan only during those periods or when they are newly eligible for Medicare. (Beneficiaries who receive low-income subsidies can change their plan at any time.) CBO found that between 2007 and 2010, about a quarter of beneficiaries in stand-alone plans joined a new plan each year. In addition, about a third of beneficiaries who joined a new plan each year were new to the program and enrolling in a plan for the first time, while the other two-thirds were switching from other stand-alone plans—which had higher premiums, on average, than the new plan they joined.[31]

Federal Payments

Federal payments are set to cover about 75 percent of the average cost of the basic drug benefit, and beneficiaries' premiums cover the remainder. A small part of that 75 percent subsidy on the basic benefit is offset by a surcharge levied on beneficiaries whose income exceeds a certain threshold. The federal government's payments take several forms:

- Direct subsidy payments are based on the bids of all plans and do not vary depending on an enrollee's choice of plans: Enrollees who choose a more expensive plan pay a premium that is correspondingly higher, and enrollees who choose a less expensive plan keep the resulting savings. Lower bids by plans, weighted by enrollment, translate into lower payments by the federal government (see Appendix A).
- Reinsurance payments are based on actual drug costs and cover 80 percent of an enrollee's spending once it exceeds a catastrophic threshold ($4,550 in 2014). The reinsurance payments combined with the direct subsidy payments are designed to cover about 75 per-cent of the average cost of the basic benefit. Those reinsurance payments greatly limit plans' costs for enrollees with high drug spending, but they also reduce plans' incentives to control spending for those enrollees.
- Subsidies to low-income beneficiaries cover the enrollee's premium, up to a maximum amount. The maximum premium subsidy, commonly called the low-income benchmark, is determined annually for each Part D region and is designed to provide low-income beneficiaries with a variety of plan choices for which their premium is zero. Low-income beneficiaries who select a plan with a premium above the low-income benchmark pay the difference between the benchmark and the plan's premium.
- Subsidies to low-income beneficiaries also cover most cost-sharing amounts. For all plans, most low-income beneficiaries make small copayments, ranging from about $1 to $3 per prescription for generic drugs and about $4 to $6 per prescription for brand-name drugs in 2014.
- Payments to plans are adjusted in ways that are designed to encourage plan sponsors to participate in the program and to address problems that sometimes arise in health insurance markets. For example, the government's payments to each plan are adjusted for the specific health conditions of the beneficiaries enrolled in that plan (a procedure known as risk adjustment). That mechanism compensates plans that attract a large number of beneficiaries whose medical conditions raise their expected drug costs, and it reduces the incentive

for plans to selectively market themselves to beneficiaries who they believe will be healthy and therefore less expensive to insure.

CBO's analysis of plans' bids defined those bids as they are specified in the law—that is, a bid equals the amount the plan is willing to accept to provide the basic benefit to a beneficiary of average health *minus* the amount the plan expects to be paid in the form of reinsurance.

Competition and Plan Bidding

The competitive pressure on plans in Medicare Part D is stronger when more plan sponsors compete in a region.[32] Between 2006 and 2007, the number of plan sponsors offering stand-alone plans in the Part D program increased from an average of 16 competitors per region to an average of 22 competitors. Many of the plan sponsors that offered a stand-alone drug plan for the first time in 2007 had offered a drug plan in 2006 as part of a Medicare Advantage plan. In 2008, the number of plan sponsors per region fell to 18, on average, and remained there through 2010. Plan sponsors who exited particular regional markets tended to be those that were purchased by another plan sponsor or had low enrollment; new plan sponsors also joined some markets during each year of the analysis.

After controlling for a variety of other factors, CBO found that between 2007 and 2010, plan sponsors in regions with more competitors submitted lower bids for basic stand-alone plans. Specifically, statistical analyses conducted by CBO under several modeling specifications found that having an additional plan sponsor in a region was correlated with an average reduction in bids of 20 cents to 50 cents per enrollee per month among plans with a premium above the low-income benchmark in the previous year.[33] That reduction represents about half a percent of the average bid for that subset of plans. Conversely, having one fewer plan sponsor in a region was associated with an average increase in bids of 20 cents to 50 cents per enrollee per month among such plans. (The economic theory of auctions and some models of price competition predict that as the number of competitors in a market increases, prices fall by less for each additional competitor. Consistent with that theory, CBO found that adding one plan sponsor in a market with 20 sponsors was associated with bids that were about 10 cents lower than when a sponsor was added to a market with only 15 sponsors.) According to that estimate, if the number of plan sponsors had not fallen between 2007 and

2010, the corresponding reduction in bids would have saved the government between $30 million and $70 million in 2010 (or about 0.1 percent of net federal spending on Part D).[34]

To further lower the government's costs for Part D by fostering greater competition between plan sponsors, the government could try to develop policies that would increase the average number of sponsors per region. However, it is unclear which policies would have that effect (apart from policies that simply raised total payments to plans, which would increase the government's costs). Alternatively, the government could adjust policies to make it easier for plans with low bids to attract beneficiaries, which would increase the incentive for plan sponsors to set low bids. For example, the government could send information to beneficiaries about the cost of their plan and other plans offered in their region during the open-enrollment period.[35] Or the government could require that all beneficiaries actively reaffirm their choice of plan, select a new plan every few years, or be reassigned to a low-cost plan in their region that covered the drugs they have been taking (not all plans cover all drugs); those sorts of changes in policy would increase the likelihood that beneficiaries would select low-cost plans, although it might also cause some inconvenience to beneficiaries or even lead them to exit the program.

Program Features That Reduce Incentives to Bid Low

Even though the Medicare Part D program was generally designed to encourage competition between plan sponsors on the basis of plans' premiums, certain aspects of the program dampen the incentive to submit lower bids. In particular, the rules for low-income beneficiaries and catastrophic drug coverage, as well as other features of the program that reduce plans' risks, lessen the incentives for plans to constrain drug spending and keep their bids and premiums low. Those elements of Part D reflect trade-offs made by policymakers to achieve the multiple goals of protecting low-income beneficiaries from financial hardship, encouraging plan sponsors to participate in the Part D market, and holding down the government's costs.

Rules for Low-Income Beneficiaries

Two aspects of Part D's rules for low-income beneficiaries—the way in which their premiums are set and the way in which they are assigned to plans—reduce the incentive for plan sponsors to submit low bids.

First, most low-income beneficiaries who select a plan with a premium below the low-income benchmark set by the government pay no premium for Part D coverage; the government pays their premium (as well as some of their cost-sharing amounts). However, if those beneficiaries select a plan with a premium above the benchmark, they are required to pay any difference between the plan's premium and the benchmark. Accordingly, most low-income beneficiaries have an incentive to select a plan with a premium below the benchmark but have no incentive to select lower-cost plans among the plans that meet that criterion.

Second, the rules for assigning some low-income beneficiaries to plans do not distinguish among plans whose premiums are below the benchmark. Specifically, beneficiaries who are already covered by Medicaid when they become eligible for Medicare are randomly assigned to a Part D plan with a premium below the benchmark if they do not actively choose a plan themselves, and low-income beneficiaries who have been assigned to a plan whose premium subsequently exceeds the benchmark are reassigned randomly to one of the plans with a premium below the benchmark.[36] Between 2007 and 2010, 1 million to 2 million low-income beneficiaries a year were automatically reassigned to plans with premiums below the low-income benchmark for their region, and they were assigned evenly across those plans regardless of the extent to which the plans' premiums were below the benchmarks. Plans with premiums below the benchmarks received an average of 4,000 new beneficiaries each year through that process; in some regions and years, such plans received more than 15,000 new beneficiaries.

For both of those reasons, plans with the lowest premiums do not end up with more beneficiaries than plans with higher premiums that are still below the bench-mark—but their lower bids cause them to receive smaller payments. Therefore, if a plan was designed to appeal mainly to low-income beneficiaries or to serve primarily new beneficiaries who were automatically reassigned, that plan's sponsor would have an incentive to submit a bid for the plan that caused its premium to be just below the benchmark but not any lower. Such strategic planning was made easier because the benchmark in each region rarely fell after 2007 and when it did, fell by only a few dollars from year to year; most benchmarks have risen by a few dollars per year since 2007.[37]

The share of enrollees in plans with premiums below the benchmark who received the low-income subsidy increased from an average of 70 percent in the first few years of the program to 90 percent by 2009. Because beneficiaries in those plans tended not to be sensitive to an increase in the plans' premiums and because those plans already offered premiums on the lower end of the range in those regions, the plans could raise their premiums toward the benchmarks without losing many enrollees. Over the 2007–2010 period, plans with a premium below the benchmark in the previous year increased their bid by an amount related to their distance below the benchmark. For example, a plan with a premium $10 below the benchmark in the previous year increased its bid by $8.30 in the subsequent year, all else being equal, CBO estimated. That increase was proportionately larger for plans with bids closer to the benchmark. Moreover, the bids of plans that received low-income enrollees through the automatic assignment process were less sensitive to the number of competing sponsors than were the bids of plans that did not receive low-income enrollees.

Shielding low-income beneficiaries from the costs of prescription drugs is an important objective for some policy-makers, and the design of the Part D program reflects the trade-off between that objective and a desire to hold down costs to the government. The rules of the program could be altered, however, in ways that would continue to protect low-income beneficiaries but would also lower bids and government spending. For example, the government could adopt a reassignment mechanism that preferentially assigned low-income beneficiaries to the plans with premiums furthest below the benchmark; that approach would provide a stronger incentive to plans to submit low bids and would reduce the government's spending even if plans did not alter their bids.[38] Such a change, however, would probably need to be combined with a change in how the low-income benchmark was calculated. The current calculation weights bids by the number of low-income beneficiaries in each plan; as a result, if all low-income beneficiaries were reassigned to plans with premiums in the lowest 25 percent of premiums in a region, the benchmark in the next year would fall such that the number of plans that qualified for reassignment would be much smaller.

Rules for Catastrophic Drug Coverage

When a plan's spending for a beneficiary in Part D exceeds a catastrophic threshold, the federal government reimburses the plan for 80 percent of that beneficiary's drug spending above the threshold, and the beneficiary pays 5 percent of drug spending above the threshold. Thus, plans need to include in their bids only 15 percent of expected spending above the threshold, and plans are at risk for only 15 percent of the difference between actual spending above the catastrophic threshold and the amount of spending estimated when the plans submitted their bids. That diminished risk tempers plans' incentives to hold down drug spending.[39]

The rules for catastrophic drug coverage reflect a trade-off between policymakers' interest in protecting plans from the consequences of enrolling a disproportionate share of high-cost beneficiaries and their desire to create strong incentives for plans to restrain drug spending and thereby hold down costs to the government.[40] Below the initial coverage limit ($2,850 in 2014), plans bear most of the risk if spending on drugs differs from expectations. By reducing the risk borne by plans when spending exceeds the catastrophic threshold, policymakers expected that more plans would enter the market and be less averse to enrolling beneficiaries with potentially high costs. (When the Medicare Modernization Act was enacted, private insurance companies did not generally offer stand-alone drug coverage.)

The government could strengthen the incentive for plans to better manage catastrophic drug spending by increasing the share of that spending for which the plans were responsible (and thus would factor into their bids). Under the law, the combination of direct subsidies and reinsurance covers about 75 percent of the cost of the basic benefit (with beneficiaries' premiums covering the remainder). If the law was changed to shift costs from reinsurance into plans' bids, reinsurance costs would fall but direct subsidies would increase, and the total government subsidy of about 75 percent of costs for the basic benefit would not change. However, such a modification might result in fewer new plan sponsors entering the market and greater efforts by plans to avoid higher-cost enrollees.

Other Features That Lower Plans' Risks

Part D includes other features that reflect the trade-off between encouraging plans to participate in the program by mitigating their financial risk and strengthening incentives for plans to control costs. The net effect of those features on the government's spending for Part D is not clear: Implementing weaker incentives for plans to control costs tends to push up bids and therefore increase the government's spending, but lessening plans' risks tends to boost the number of plan sponsors in each market and therefore decrease bids and the government's spending.

One feature that lowers plans' risks is risk corridor payments. Plans that spend more on drugs than they anticipated by at least a specified amount receive payments from the government that cover part of those extra costs; similarly, plans that spend less on drugs than they anticipated by at least a specified amount pay the government part of those savings. Those risk corridor payments reduce a plan's exposure to higher-than-anticipated drug spending but also decrease a plan's gain from lower-than-anticipated drug spending. Consequently, such payments weaken the incentive for plans to aggressively reduce drug spending. Recognizing that trade-off, policymakers designed a risk corridor system that had narrow corridors for the first two years of the Part D program, when plans were more uncertain about their costs, and wider corridors thereafter. By expanding the risk corridors, policy-makers lessened somewhat the adverse effects of risk corridors on plans' incentives to hold down drug costs.[41]

A second feature that reduces plans' risks is a risk-adjustment mechanism. That mechanism assigns each beneficiary a risk score—based on the person's medical conditions and demographic characteristics—that represents the expected drug costs for that person relative to the national average for the Medicare population. A beneficiary with a risk score of 1.0 has average expected costs. Plans receive proportionally larger or smaller payments from the government for their beneficiaries who are in worse or better health than average. However, research has shown that the risk-adjustment mechanism used for Part D before 2011 did not fully reimburse plans for beneficiaries with worse health than average (and tended to overcompensate plans for beneficiaries with better health than average); thus, despite the risk-adjustment mechanism, plans still had an incentive to attract beneficiaries with better health than average.[42] In 2011, to address those problems, program administrators updated the risk-adjustment formula; the new formula appears to capture the effect of health status on drug spending more accurately than the one used previously.[43]

How Payments That Plans Receive for the Basic Benefit Compare with Their Drug Spending

Between 2007 and 2010, net payments per person to Medicare Part D plans for the basic drug benefit increased faster than the plans' spending per person on drugs, CBO estimates. That finding implies that the sum of administrative costs and profits for plans increased between those years.

For each enrollee in a Part D plan, the federal government pays a direct subsidy to the plan and the enrollee pays a premium, the sum of which equals the plan's bid (after adjusting for the health of the enrollee). Together, those payments account for about 70 percent of total payments to plans. In addition, the federal government makes reinsurance payments for drug costs incurred in the catastrophic phase of the benefit; they account for the remaining roughly 30 percent of total payments to plans. In addition, plans that have lower drug spending than estimated in their bid by a certain amount are required to make risk corridor payments to the government, while plans that have higher drug spending than estimated by a corresponding amount receive risk corridor payments from the government.

CBO analyzed the payments to stand-alone Part D plans and the costs incurred by those plans in each year from 2007 through 2010. The sum of direct subsidies and premiums grew at an average annual rate of 2.2 percent per person between 2007 and 2010, and reinsurance payments to plans grew at an average annual rate of 7.5 percent per person (see Table 2-1 on page 22). In each year of that period except 2008, drug spending fell far enough below the amount predicted in plans' bids, on average, that plans paid the government between $12 and $33 per person, on net, through the risk corridor pro-gram. (In 2008, plans received payments of $6 per person from the government, on average.) In total, net payments to plans for the basic benefit grew at an average annual rate of 3.3 percent per person from 2007 to 2010. The spending by plans for drugs for the basic benefit (net of rebates) rose more slowly, at an average annual rate of 2.8 percent per person between 2007 and 2010. The difference between net payments and net drug spending, which equals the sum of administrative costs and profits, rose at an average annual rate of 6.7 percent per person between 2007 and 2010 (see Figure 2-1). CBO did not have data that enabled it to identify separate amounts for administrative costs and profits. Determining the reasons that the sum of administrative costs and profits grew faster than drug spending for the basic benefit under the Part D program is difficult given the short time the program has been operating and a lack of information about whether the initial amounts of profits and administrative costs were unusually low. For example, profits earned in 2007 may have been unusually low—perhaps because plan sponsors initially sought to submit low bids in order to capture a greater share of the market—and the faster rate of growth afterward could just indicate a return to competitive levels of profit. In addition, administrative costs may have been unusually low at first, although one might have expected those costs to be especially high at the beginning owing to various start-up costs.

Alternatively, some of the increase in the sum of profits and administrative costs might be explained by the reduction in the number of plan sponsors, and the associated increase in bids, between 2007 and 2010. Based on CBO's analysis of the association between the number of plan sponsors and plans' bids, the reduction in the number of plan sponsors could explain about 13 percent of the increase in administrative costs and profits per beneficiary over the 2007–2010 period.[44]

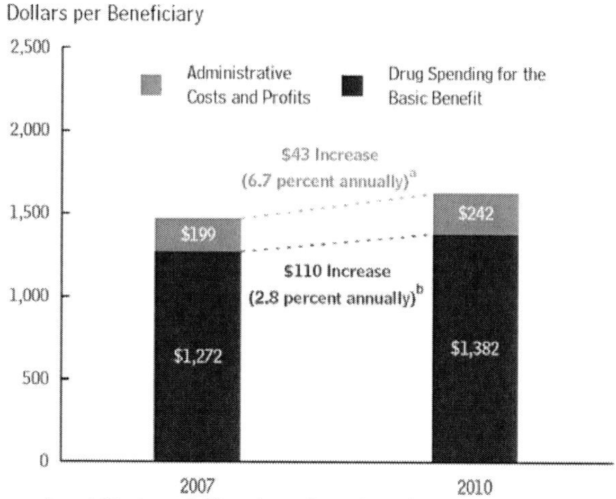

Source: Congressional Budget Office based on data from the Centers for Medicare & Medicaid Services.

a. Amounts are net of risk corridor payments, which are payments to (or from) the federal government when plans overestimate (or underestimate) their spending relative to actual spending beyond a threshold amount.

b. Amounts are net of rebates.

Figure 2-1. Changes in Costs per Beneficiary for the Basic Benefit in Stand-Alone Part D Plans between 2007 and 2010.

Table 2-1. Revenues and Costs for Stand-Alone Plans Providing the Basic Benefit under Part D, 2007 to 2010

	2007	2008	2009	2010	Average Increase per Year (Percent)
	Revenues				
Direct Subsidies and Premiums					
In dollars per person	1,064	1,046	1,111	1,136	2.2
As a percentage of total net payments to plans	72.3	68.6	70.6	70.0	n.a.

Table 2-1. (Continued)

	2007	2008	2009	2010	Average Increase per Year (Percent)
Reinsurance					
In dollars per person	419	474	492	521	7.5
As a percentage of total net payments to plans	28.5	31.1	31.2	32.1	n.a.
Risk Corridor Payments					
In dollars per person	-12	6	-29	-33	n.a.
As a percentage of total net payments to plans	-0.8	0.4	-1.8	-2.0	n.a.
Total Revenues (Dollars per person)	**1,471**	**1,526**	**1,574**	**1,624**	**3.3**
	Costs				
Net Drug Spending for the Basic Benefit[a]					
In dollars per person	1,272	1,333	1,348	1,382	2.8
As a percentage of total costs	86.5	87.4	85.7	85.1	n.a.
Administrative Costs and Profits Net of Risk Corridor Payments[b]					
In dollars per person	199	193	226	242	6.7
As a percentage of total costs	13.5	12.6	14.3	14.9	n.a.
Total Costs (Dollars per person)	**1,471**	**1,526**	**1,574**	**1,624**	**3.3**

Source: Congressional Budget Office based on data from the Centers for Medicare & Medicaid Services (CMS).

Notes: Risk corridor payments are payments made to (or from) the federal government when plans overestimate (or underestimate) their spending relative to actual spending beyond a threshold amount. All payments are credited to the benefit year in which they were incurred, even if actual payments were received in subsequent years. For a description of the basic benefit, see Box 2-1 on page 14.

n.a. = not applicable.

a. Net drug spending for the basic benefit includes plans' share of drug spending and reinsurance, after accounting for rebates. Using data for stand-alone Part D plans, CBO calculated net spending by subtracting total rebates received by plans from drug manufacturers (available from CMS) from the total amount that plans paid to pharmacies for spending attributable to the basic benefit (available from Part D claims data). Following the methodology used in the Medicare trustees' report for calculating per-person values, CBO divided net spending by total enrollment in stand-alone plans in July of each year to calculate net drug spending per person.

b. Administrative costs and profits net of risk corridor payments are equal to total plan payments minus net drug spending for the basic benefit.

SECTION 3. COMPARING MEDICARE PART D AND MEDICAID FEE FOR SERVICE

After Medicare Part D, the largest government program for delivering prescription drug benefits is Medicaid. In 2010, about 90 percent of Medicaid's drug benefits (in dollar terms) were provided through the fee-for-service (FFS) portion of Medicaid, which is administered by state Medicaid agencies.[45] For simplicity, in this report, references to Medicaid are to that FFS program.

Medicare Part D and Medicaid use different approaches to contain drug prices and thus drug spending. (Throughout this section, unless otherwise indicated, price refers to the price net of rebates.) The competitive structure of Part D gives plan sponsors significant incentives to hold down spending, as discussed in Section 2. To achieve that goal, plan sponsors use three main approaches: They encourage the use of less expensive brand-name drugs, they negotiate lower prices for brand-name drugs, and they encourage the use of generic drugs. Those approaches involve influencing the behavior of beneficiaries and their doctors as well as bargaining with retail pharmacies and manufacturers of brand-name drugs to obtain lower prices net of rebates (or discounts). By comparison, Medicaid holds down spending in two broad ways. First, the program uses an administered pricing policy, whereby drug prices are reduced relative to manufacturers' average prices mostly through rebates that are set in federal law (rather than negotiated, as in Part D).[46] Second, state governments—which pay a significant share of the program's costs—have adopted a variety of strategies to control spending.

Both approaches can contain spending to some extent under certain circumstances but are less successful at doing so under other circumstances (and may have other disadvantages as well). For example, under a competitive design, the incentive to limit spending in a market with only a few plan sponsors or a falling number of plan sponsors may be weak or decreasing. (The impact on bids of the number of plan sponsors in a Part D region is described in Section 2.) As another example, programs with administered pricing, like Medicaid, may not be able to adjust quickly to changing market conditions. Although Medicaid's statutory rebates represent a relatively flexible approach to administered pricing because of their link to market prices, effective implementation of the rebates can still present difficulties. Suppose that certain drugs were taken primarily by beneficiaries who were covered under programs that used such rebates; in that case, manufacturers of those drugs would have a strong incentive to raise their launch prices above what they would otherwise charge to offset the required rebates— potentially eliminating most savings from the rebate program for those drugs.

For this analysis, the Congressional Budget Office com-pared the average prices of drugs used in Part D and Medicaid. (Total drug spending also depends on the quantity of drugs used, but analyzing any differences in quantities in the two programs is beyond the scope of this report.) The average price of drugs in each program depends on three factors. The first factor is nationwide influences that are common to both programs—such as, in recent years, the expiration of patents on existing brand-name drugs and lower rates of entry for new brand-name drugs, as discussed in Section 1. The second factor is the prevalence of different health conditions in the populations covered by the programs, which CBO attempted to control for indirectly in its analysis. The third factor is the approaches of the programs to containing drug spending—in particular, the actions taken by plan sponsors in Part D and the statutory rebates and actions taken by states in Medicaid. To the extent that CBO's analysis controlled effectively for differences in health conditions between the populations covered by the programs, the remaining difference in the average prices of drugs used in Part D and Medicaid reflects the relative effectiveness of the approaches used by the programs to contain drug prices.

For the drug classes representing the great majority of drug spending by Part D beneficiaries, CBO found that Medicaid's average price of drugs was between 27 percent and 38 percent lower than Part D's average price in 2010 after controlling for differences in health conditions between beneficiaries of the programs. CBO expects that the difference in average prices will narrow over time as drug manufacturers respond to new rules that increased Medicaid's rebates beginning in 2010 but that Medicaid's average price will remain at least 20 percent to 30 percent lower than Part D's average price after controlling for differences in beneficiaries' health conditions.

Which end of those ranges more appropriately characterizes the relative effectiveness of the approaches used by Part D and Medicaid to contain spending depends on the extent to which differences in drug use within therapeutic classes—that is, within groups of drugs that are intended to treat common sets of medical conditions and that typically have similar modes of action—arise from differences in health conditions versus differences in the structure of the programs. The difference in average drug prices between Part D and Medicaid in 2010 occurred primarily because Medicaid's statutory rebates on brand-name drugs were generally much larger than the rebates on those drugs negotiated by plan sponsors in Part D. Rates of generic drug use were similar in the two pro-grams, so the higher prices paid by Part D for brand-name drugs were not offset by significantly greater use of generic drugs. However, the higher prices for given brand-name drugs were offset in part by greater use of lower-priced drugs within therapeutic classes in Part D. If the different patterns of use within therapeutic classes stemmed entirely from differences in the structure of the programs, then the lower end of those ranges—27 percent in 2010 and at least 20 percent in the future— reflects the relative effectiveness of those program structures in containing drug prices. If, instead, the different patterns of use within therapeutic classes stemmed entirely from differences in health conditions between beneficiaries of the programs, then the higher end of those ranges—38 percent in 2010 and at least 30 percent in the future—reflects the relative effectiveness of those program structures in containing drug prices.

Some policymakers have proposed applying Medicaid's statutory rebates to drug purchases made by Part D beneficiaries who receive low-income subsidies (while retaining the existing structure of Part D in other respects). CBO expects that adopting such a policy would lower the average cost of brand-name drugs in Part D and thus reduce the federal government's costs over the first decade after the policy was adopted. But a substantial portion of those savings would probably erode over time because drug manufacturers would counter the larger rebates by raising the prices for new brand-name drugs. In addition, that policy would reduce the incentive for firms to develop new drugs.

How Medicare Part D Contains Drug Spending

The competitive design of the Part D program creates incentives for plans to efficiently manage drug benefits in order to hold down bids and premiums and attract enrollees. Part D plan sponsors primarily use three closely related techniques to achieve those objectives:

- *Steering Beneficiaries and Their Doctors by Using a Tiered Formulary*. Plan sponsors develop formularies (lists of covered drugs) for their plans in which some drugs are in preferred tiers with lower copayments and other drugs are in nonpreferred tiers with higher copayments. That structure encourages beneficiaries to choose lower-priced drugs. In addition, plan sponsors sometimes require doctors to justify prescribing higher-priced drugs.

- *Negotiating Rebates That Lower Prices of Certain Brand-Name Drugs.* Plan sponsors often pay lower prices for brand-name drugs from manufacturers in exchange for steering beneficiaries toward those drugs by placing them in preferred tiers.
- *Encouraging the Use of Generic Drugs.* Plan sponsors encourage beneficiaries to use generic drugs by setting lower copayments for those drugs. The greater use of generic drugs that results from that incentive reflects both substitution of generic drugs for their brand-name counterparts and substitution of drug therapies that offer generic alternatives for therapies that have only a brand-name version available.

Steering Beneficiaries and Their Doctors by Using a Tiered Formulary

Part D plan sponsors can encourage beneficiaries to use lower-cost drugs by creating preferred and nonpreferred tiers for brand-name drugs within their formularies. Lower copayments for drugs in the preferred tiers and higher copayments for drugs in the nonpreferred tiers encourage the use of those preferred drugs. (As explained below, generic drugs are typically placed in a separate tier with even lower copayments.) Although doctors generally determine which drug is appropriate for a patient, patients have an incentive to ask about or request alternatives when they face differing copayments.

Most Part D plans have tiered formularies with different copayments for each tier, sometimes using four or five tiers. In addition to the preferred and nonpreferred tiers for brand-name drugs, plans tend to steer beneficiaries away from the most expensive drugs—those with a retail price that exceeds $600 per prescription—by placing those drugs on a "specialty tier" for which out-of-pocket costs can be more than four times as high as for preferred drugs. Plans may also require prior authorization before drugs from the specialty tier are dispensed, or they may require that beneficiaries try generic substitutes or less expensive brand-name drugs before a more expensive brand-name drug is approved (a practice known as step therapy).[47] Under those approaches, enrollees have an incentive to ask physicians who prescribe specialty drugs to justify the use of those costlier drugs. In 2010, across all plans that used multiple tiers to segment brand-name drugs, CBO found that about 70 percent of beneficiaries' spending on brand-name drugs was for drugs on the preferred tiers of their plans; about 19 percent was for drugs on the nonpreferred tiers; and about 10 percent was for drugs on the specialty tier.

Researchers suggest that the negotiating leverage gained by plan sponsors because of their plans' ability to steer beneficiaries to particular drugs has, on average, con-strained the rate of growth in drug prices more for drugs for which Medicare constitutes a larger share of the drug's market.[48] In some instances, however, the ability of Part D plans to use their formularies to encourage beneficiaries to use less expensive brand-name drugs is limited by the statutory design of the program. For example, subsidies that cover cost sharing for most low-income beneficiaries require those beneficiaries to pay a small fixed amount for all brand-name drugs, regardless of whether those drugs receive preferred placement on a plan's formulary. That design reflects the trade-off made by policymakers between limiting potential out-of-pocket costs for low-income beneficiaries and constraining government spending.

Negotiating Rebates That Lower Prices of Certain Brand-Name Drugs

The ability to steer beneficiaries toward preferred drugs gives Part D plan sponsors leverage when negotiating drug prices. Negotiation for drug prices within Part D occurs between plan sponsors and pharmacies for retail prices and between plan sponsors and manufacturers of brand-name drugs for additional rebates. Manufacturers would have no incentive to pay rebates if beneficiaries would use their drugs anyway, so they tend to offer the largest rebates to plan sponsors that actively steer large shares of beneficiaries to their drugs.[49] Plan sponsors steer beneficiaries primarily by charging lower copayments for certain drugs than for others. Steering beneficiaries through copayment differentials is easiest when the drugs within a therapeutic class are close substitutes, because the probability that a beneficiary's doctor will prescribe a close substitute is relatively high; thus, rebates tend to be higher in therapeutic classes containing more drugs that are close substitutes.

Plan sponsors face some constraints in using differing copayments to steer drug use, however, particularly for drugs used by low-income beneficiaries. One approach used in some plans is to exclude from their formularies altogether some drugs that would otherwise appear on a nonpreferred tier. That approach might be particularly attractive for plans that primarily serve low-income beneficiaries, because of the constraints on copayments for covered drugs. But a plan's ability to exclude drugs is limited because, by law and regulation, a plan must cover at least two drugs in each therapeutic class and all (or nearly all) drugs in six designated classes.[50] Even so, that approach may have enabled some plan sponsors to negotiate large rebates for certain drugs used by low-income beneficiaries by limiting coverage of some other drugs sold at higher prices.[51]

Encouraging the Use of Generic Drugs

Part D plan sponsors have also reduced costs by steering beneficiaries toward generic drugs instead of brand-name drugs. The primary way in which Part D plan sponsors accomplish that goal is by creating within their formularies a "generic tier" with lower copayments for generic drugs. Another way in which Part D plan sponsors sometimes steer beneficiaries toward generic drugs is by excluding brand-name drugs from coverage when generic counterparts are available.

How Medicaid FFS Contains Drug Spending

To contain drug spending, Medicaid uses two types of statutory rebates on drug purchases and a variety of actions by state governments, which administer the program.

The two statutory rebates on brand-name drugs in Med-icaid together averaged 57 percent of manufacturers' average prices in 2010. Those rebates operate as follows:

- The "basic rebate" requires manufacturers to offer a discount on their brand-name drugs that is at least 23.1 percent of the average manufacturer's price—that is, the price that manufacturers receive before rebates for sales through retail pharmacies.[52] (The 23.1 percent figure is thus referred to here as the "minimum rebate.") If, however, the manufacturer offers any "qualified" purchaser in the private sector a rebate in excess of 23.1 percent, then the rebate received by Medicaid is increased to match that larger private rebate. Qualified purchasers in this case include many private-sector purchasers—such as hospitals, mail-order pharmacies, and health maintenance organizations—but exclude pharmacy benefit managers, Medicare Part D drug plans, and most other government purchasers. To enforce those requirements, manufacturers are required to report to the Centers for Medicare & Medicaid Services the lowest price paid for their drug after accounting for any rebate—known as the "best price"—if they want Medicaid to cover their drug.[53]

- The "inflation rebate" is imposed if the average manufacturer's price for a brand-name drug rises faster than general inflation, as measured by the consumer price index for all urban consumers (CPI-U). The average manufacturer's price and the average retail price of brand-name drugs typically rise faster than the CPI-U. For example, between 2007 and 2010, the average retail price of brand-name drugs in Part D increased by 8.5 percent per year, on average, whereas the CPI-U increased by 1.7 percent per year, on average. (For brand-name drugs, the retail price tends to track the manufacturer's price but to be slightly higher.) The inflation rebate represents about half of the total rebates for brand-name drugs in Medicaid.

Because Medicaid beneficiaries have low income, their copayments for drugs are set by law and regulation to be quite small. In 2014, for example, copayments were generally about $1 to $4 per prescription and covered less than 5 percent of total drug costs. The remaining costs of drugs are divided between the federal government, which pays about 60 percent, on average, and state governments, which pay about 40 percent, on average. Thus, state governments have a significant incentive to contain drug spending. To achieve that goal, state Medicaid agencies commonly use four techniques:

- Many states encourage beneficiaries to use generic drugs by offering them at slightly lower copayments than apply to brand-name drugs. The differences between copayments tend to be small, though, because Medicaid's copayments for prescription drugs are limited by law. That limitation protects Medicaid beneficiaries from being unable to afford to purchase certain drugs, but it also reduces the ability of states to use copayments to encourage beneficiaries to choose less expensive drugs. The limit on copayment differentials in Medicaid is similar to that in the Part D benefit for low-income enrollees.
- States' payments to pharmacies for drugs that are available in both a brand-name version and a generic version are usually based on the cost of the generic drug plus a dispensing fee. For that reason, pharmacies have strong financial incentives to fill prescriptions using generic versions when those are available and when the prescription allows for generic substitution.
- Some states limit the use of drugs by capping the number of prescriptions that can be dispensed per month per beneficiary. In

2010, four states placed such limits on brand-name prescriptions.[54] Those limits reduced the overall quantity of drugs used and increased the share of prescriptions filled with generic drugs. Another 14 states placed such limits on the total number of prescriptions (both brand-name and generic) per beneficiary.[55] Those limits reduced the overall quantity of drugs used but also probably decreased the share of Medicaid-paid prescriptions filled with generic drugs, because some beneficiaries subject to the limit probably filled their prescriptions for brand-name drugs within the Medicaid program and used their own funds to pay for the less-expensive generic drugs. The remaining 32 states and the District of Columbia, which accounted for about 40 percent of total Medicaid drug spending in 2010, did not limit the number of prescriptions per beneficiary.

- Many states engage in negotiations with manufacturers to receive supplemental rebates. Manufacturers agree to pay those supplemental rebates on some brand-name drugs in exchange for states' not requiring a beneficiary's physician to obtain approval from a state entity before a pharmacy can dispense those drugs. Such prior-authorization requirements tend to reduce sales of the affected drugs.

Federal law prohibits state Medicaid agencies from taking certain measures to contain drug spending. For example, states may not exclude specific drugs, such as high-cost drugs, from coverage. (Private managed care organizations serving Medicaid beneficiaries, by contrast, have a greater ability to actively manage drug use by, for instance, excluding certain drugs from coverage.) Also, states cannot require significantly higher copayments for more expensive drugs.

Comparing Average Drug Prices in Medicare Part D and Medicaid

Medicare Part D and Medicaid differ in the prices they pay for drugs because the tools they use to restrain drug spending have differing effects on three variables: the rebates each program receives for the same brand-name drugs, the rate of generic drug use observed in each program, and the shares of drugs used with higher and lower prices within each therapeutic class. The average prices paid for drugs in the two programs also differ because differences in the health conditions of the beneficiaries of the programs lead to different mixes of drugs being pre-scribed. After controlling indirectly for health conditions (in a manner described below), CBO found that the Medicaid program paid significantly lower prices in 2010 than Part D plans paid, primarily because Medicaid's statutory rebates exceeded the rebates negotiated by plan sponsors in Part D.[56]

The following subsections report the results of CBO's analysis for each of the key variables listed—rebates, generic drug use, and the use of drugs within therapeutic classes—and then for prices overall; key caveats about the analysis are examined at the end of the section.

Differences in Rebates

CBO estimated that the average rebate negotiated between Part D plan sponsors and manufacturers of brand-name drugs was 15 percent of retail prices in 2010, up from 12 percent in 2007. That estimate was based on all active ingredients used by Part D beneficiaries. Several of the findings in this analysis are based on the active ingredients present in the top 53 therapeutic classes of drugs, which accounted for 70 percent of Part D spending in 2010 (see Appendix B for more information). For those active ingredients, the average Part D rebate on brand-name drugs was 17 percent in 2010, CBO found.

That rebate is much smaller than the average rebate received by Medicaid. CBO estimated that in 2010, Medicaid's average rebate on all brand-name drugs (comprising the basic rebate and the inflation rebate) was 54 percent of retail prices; for brand-name drugs in the top 53 therapeutic classes, Medicaid's average rebate was 56 percent.

Differences in the Use of Generic Drugs

The rate of generic drug use in Part D is similar to that in Medicaid, CBO found, which suggests that the tools used by those programs to encourage the use of generic drugs are about equally effective. For each of the top 53 therapeutic classes, CBO estimated the rate of generic drug use for Part D and for Medicaid; CBO then averaged rates across the 53 classes for each program using weights that matched the use of each class in Part D. Using weights based on use in Part D leads to estimates of generic drug use in Medicaid *as if* Medicaid beneficiaries were similar to Part D beneficiaries in their health conditions and in the consequent availability across drug classes of generic drugs to treat those conditions (see Appendix B for more information).

For the therapeutic classes CBO analyzed, the rate of generic drug use in 2010 was 75 percent within Part D and 70 percent within Medicaid (see Table

3-1). Despite the rough similarity of those overall percentages, though, the use of generic drugs in Part D and Medicaid differed substantially for many individual classes of drugs (see Table B-1 on page 41). The rate of generic drug use also varied among certain subsets of beneficiaries in the programs:

- For beneficiaries in states that cap the total number of prescriptions covered by Medicaid, claims data may understate true generic use because beneficiaries may choose to fill their prescriptions for brand-name drugs through Medicaid and their prescriptions for less-expensive generic drugs outsidc of the program. CBO estimated that in 2010, the average rate of generic drug use in Medicaid was 67 percent in states with caps and 74 percent in states without caps.

  Stand-alone drug plans within Medicare Part D probably offer a closer comparison to Medicaid than Medicare Advantage prescription drug (MAPD) plans do, because (like Medicaid) the stand-alone plans provide a drug benefit that is administered separately from enrollees' other medical benefits. CBO estimated that in 2010, the rate of generic drug use was 73 percent among Part D stand-alone plans and 77 percent among Medicare Advantage plans. Low-income enrollees in stand-alone plans may provide an even closer comparison to Medicaid because they have limited resources and face low copayments for drugs (as Medicaid beneficiaries do); the rate of generic drug use among low-income enrollees in stand-alone plans in 2010 was 73 percent.
- Enrollees in MAPD plans who do not receive low-income subsidies have the highest rate of generic drug use—an estimated 78 percent in 2010—in Medicare Part D. One reason why the rate of generic use was slightly higher for beneficiaries in MAPD plans might be that those beneficiaries are usually served by physicians' and other health care providers affiliated with their plan, and steering a beneficiary toward particular drugs is easier when the plan has a relationship with the physician who is prescribing the drugs. Another reason might be that, even in the absence of such relationships, MAPD plans may have doctors in their net-works who are more likely to prescribe generic drugs.

Table 3-1. Rates of Generic Drug Use in Medicare and Medicaid, 2010

Percent			
	Low-Income Beneficiaries	**Other Beneficiaries**	**All Beneficiaries**
Use in Medicare Part D			
Stand-alone plans	73	74	73
Medicare Advantage plans	75	78	77
Total Use in Medicare Part D	74	76	75
Use in Medicaid Fee for Service			
States with no caps[a]	n.a.	n.a.	74
States with caps	n.a.	n.a.	67
Total Use in Medicaid Fee for Service	n.a.	n.a.	70

Source: Congressional Budget Office based on data from the Centers for Medicare & Medicaid Services and Red Book data (available from Truven Health Analytics) to determine whether a drug was brand-name or generic.

Notes: The use rates for generic drugs are measured as days of generic drugs supplied as shares of total days of drugs supplied and then weighted across therapeutic classes based on days supplied within Medicare Part D. The number of days supplied is estimated by multiplying the units dispensed by the days supplied per unit as estimated from Part D claims data.

n.a. = not applicable.

a. Eighteen states capped the number of prescriptions dispensed per month per beneficiary, which changed the incentive for beneficiaries to consume generic drugs within the program and thus changed the rate of generic drug use calculated for the nation as a whole.

Although CBO has sought to address disparate influences on the use of generic drugs in Part D and Medicaid, comparisons of the data presented here must still be interpreted with caution. For example, within the Medicaid program, some brand-name drugs may be cheaper than their generic counterparts after accounting for Medicaid's statutory rebates—and some states discourage generic substitution in such instances. In addition, although CBO's analysis of therapeutic classes attempts to control indirectly for differences in the prevalence of health conditions among beneficiaries in the two programs, other differences between the populations could affect their respective rates of generic drug use within a therapeutic class.

Differences in the Use of Drugs within Therapeutic Classes

CBO found that beneficiaries of Part D tend to use less expensive drugs within therapeutic classes than do beneficiaries of Medicaid. Specifically, CBO estimated that the average price of drugs within Part D would have been 15 percent higher if the mix of drugs used within therapeutic classes matched that of Medicaid rather than that of Part D, and the average price of drugs within Medicaid would have been 15 percent lower if the mix of drugs used within therapeutic classes matched that of Medicare rather than that of Medicaid.[57]

The source of that difference is unclear. On the one hand, the difference might arise because the competitive design of the Part D program creates incentives for plan sponsors to steer utilization toward lower-priced drugs in a therapeutic class through the use of formularies and differential copayments. On the other hand, the difference might arise because the prevalence of certain health conditions differs between Part D and Medicaid beneficiaries, leading the doctors of Part D beneficiaries to select less expensive drugs in a therapeutic class for nonfinancial reasons. Moreover, both explanations might be true in part. In addition, this analysis does not incorporate the effect of supplemental rebates that some states have negotiated on top of the rebates mandated by federal law, which could change the relative prices of active ingredients within therapeutic classes for Medicaid.

Overall Difference in Average Prices

The difference in the average prices paid for drugs by Part D and Medicaid depends on the differences in rebates, in the rates of generic drug use, and in the shares of drugs used with higher and lower prices within each therapeutic class. Average prices also depend on differences in the health conditions of the programs' beneficiaries, which CBO tried to account for in this analysis. Specifically, CBO estimated the difference in average prices between Part D and Medicaid for the top 53 therapeutic classes using two alternative approaches.

In one approach, the agency calculated the average price of prescription drugs within each therapeutic class for each program and then averaged across classes using weights that match the use of each class in Part D.[58] (See Appendix B for more details on CBO's methodology.) On that basis, CBO estimated that Medicaid paid $36, on average, for a 30-day supply of drugs in 2010, whereas Part D paid $49 (see Figure 3-1).[59] The difference of $13 amounts to a reduction of about one-quarter (27 percent) relative to the average price paid in Part D.

That comparison incorporates Medicaid's substantially larger average rebate on brand-name drugs (56 percent, compared with 17 percent in Part D), Medicaid's slightly lower rate of use of generic drugs (70 percent, compared with 75 percent for Part D), and Part D's greater use of lower-priced drugs within therapeutic classes (Part D prices would be 15 percent higher under Medicaid's use pattern). The comparison does not include supplemental Medicaid rebates negotiated by states, which averaged 3 percent of retail pharmacy spending in 2010; including those rebates would make the difference between drug prices under Part D and Medicaid slightly larger.

CBO also made an alternative estimate of the difference in average prices that does *not* include the effects of Part D's greater use of lower-priced drugs within therapeutic classes. To exclude those effects, CBO modified its first approach by applying weights not to therapeutic classes but instead to all of the active ingredients present in those classes, with the weights based on the use of those ingredients in Part D. That second approach shows what the mix of *active ingredients* consumed by Medicare Part D beneficiaries would have cost at Medicaid prices— in contrast to CBO's first approach, which shows what the mix of *drug classes* consumed by Medicare beneficiaries would have cost at Medicaid prices. (See Appendix B for more details.)

To understand why that alternative approach excludes the effects of Part D's use of lower-priced drugs within therapeutic classes, suppose that a therapeutic class consisted of just two drugs with different active ingredients and that Part D beneficiaries used the drug that was less expensive more often than Medicaid beneficiaries did. For CBO's first approach, a weight is applied to the class as a whole based on the use of that class in Part D relative to the use of other classes in Part D; in that case, the average price of drugs in that class used by Medicaid beneficiaries is increased relative to that of Part D beneficiaries by Medicaid beneficiaries' greater use of the more expensive drug. By contrast, for CBO's second approach, weights are applied separately to the active ingredient in each drug based on the use of that ingredient in Part D relative to the use of other ingredients in Part D; in that case, Medicaid beneficiaries' greater use of the more expensive drug has no effect on the calculation because the weights used for those drugs are the same in calculating average prices in both Part D and Medicaid.[60]

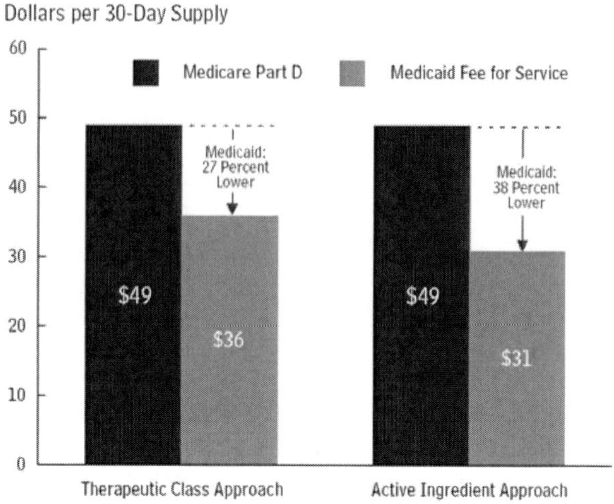

Source: Congressional Budget Office based on Medicare Part D claims data, Medicare Part D rebate data, and Medicaid fee-for-service (FFS) drug pricing, rebate, and use data obtained from the Centers for Medicare & Medicaid Services.

Notes: Prices are net of rebates. Under the therapeutic class approach, after calculating the average price of a 30-day supply within each therapeutic class (based on Medicaid or Part D use and pricing), CBO calculated a weighted average price across the 53 classes using days supplied in Part D to determine the weights applied to the classes. Under the active ingredient approach, after calculating the average price of a 30-day supply for each active ingredient (dosage form and strength) across both brand-name and any available generic forms (based on Medicaid or Part D use and pricing), CBO calculated a weighted average price across the active ingredients in the 53 classes using days supplied in Part D to determine the weights applied to the active ingredients.

CBO expects the price difference between Medicare Part D and Medicaid FFS to lessen somewhat over time as manufacturers respond to the change made in Medicaid's basic rebate in the Affordable Care Act. Other changes in the drug market over time, such as the relative use of brand-name and generic drugs, will also affect this price difference in the future.

Figure 3-1. Average Price of Drugs in 53 Therapeutic Classes in Medicare Part D and Medicaid Fee for Service, 2010.

Under that alternative approach, CBO estimated that Medicaid paid $31, on average, for a 30-day supply of drugs in the top 53 therapeutic classes in 2010, whereas Part D paid $49.[61] The difference of $18 amounts to a reduction of more than one-third (38 percent) relative to the average price paid in Part D.[62]

Which of those comparisons better reflects the effect on drug prices of the different approaches to cost containment in Part D and Medicaid is unclear. To the extent that the difference in the mix of drugs used within therapeutic classes stems from the incentives in Part D, then the reduction in average prices resulting from that different mix can be attributed to the different approaches to cost containment. In that case, the estimate that Medic-aid prices were, on average, 27 percent below Part D prices better captures the differing effects of the approaches of the two programs to contain drug costs. But to the extent that the difference in the mix of drugs within a class stems from differences in health conditions among Part D and Medicaid beneficiaries, then it should not be attributed to the different approaches to cost containment. In that case, the active ingredient estimate— that Medicaid prices were, on average, 38 percent below Part D prices—is the better measure of the differing approaches of the two programs to containing drug costs. Unfortunately, CBO does not have an analytic basis for identifying how much of the difference in the mix of drugs used within therapeutic classes can be attributed to each of those explanations.

Additional Caveats about This Analysis

Two issues deserve further explanation. First, the difference in average drug prices between Part D and Medicaid in 2010 partly reflects a legislative change that was implemented in that year under the Affordable Care Act. The basic rebate for Medicaid was increased in 2010 from 15.1 percent to 23.1 percent. CBO expects manufacturers to respond to that increase over time by raising their before-rebate prices for new drugs; those price increases will probably enable the manufacturers to regain a significant portion of the lost revenues. (Drugs already on the market are subject to Medicaid's inflation rebate, so raising the prices of those drugs does not increase manufacturers'' net revenues from sales to Medicaid.)[63] CBO also expects that as manufacturers raise the before-rebate prices of new drugs, they will increase rebates on those drugs for Part D to maintain similar net prices—because the increase in the Medicaid rebate will probably not have much effect on negotiating leverage between manufacturers and plan sponsors in Part D. Therefore, as sales of drugs that were launched after 2010 become an increasing share of total drug sales, the difference in average drug prices between Part D and Medicaid will diminish from what it was in 2010.

If manufacturers raised launch prices (before rebates) enough to entirely eliminate the effect of the higher basic rebate, Medicaid's net prices would rise by about 10 percent in real (inflation-adjusted) dollars over the next two decades, holding all else equal. That change would reduce the amount by which average Medicaid prices were below average Part D prices from 27 percent to roughly 20 percent when weighted by the use of drugs in different therapeutic classes and from 38 percent to roughly 30 percent when weighted by the use of different active ingredients. However, other factors in the drug market may lead manufacturers to offset only a portion of the higher basic rebate through higher launch prices.

Second, CBO's analysis addressed differences in the prices of drugs used in Part D and Medicaid but not differences in the quantities of drugs used. The quantities could differ because of differences in both the structures of the programs and the beneficiaries of the programs. A complete analysis of the effects of the programs' approaches to containing drug spending would need to address the effects on quantities as well as on prices—and such an analysis would need to control for differences in the incidence and severity of various medical conditions, as well as other differences between enrollees. That analysis is beyond the scope of this report.

Applying Statutory Rebates to Medicare Part D

Some policymakers have proposed that statutory rebates similar to those in Medicaid be extended to drug purchases by beneficiaries of Part D who receive low-income subsidies (while otherwise maintaining the program's existing structure). Applying such rebates to those purchases would reduce the prices paid for drugs in Part D, especially during the first decade after those rebates were established. For example, CBO has estimated that one approach to applying Medicaid-style rebates to drug purchases by low-income beneficiaries in Part D would reduce federal spending by $123 billion from 2014 to 2023.[64] Proposals of that type represent one approach to reducing the cost to the Part D program of covering low-income beneficiaries; some other approaches are discussed in Section 2.

Such proposals would have effects beyond the federal budget. In particular, because lower prices for Part D would reduce the expected return from drug development efforts and because manufacturers would face heightened uncertainty about the magnitude of future statutory rebates in Part D, CBO expects that the pace at which new drugs were developed would be reduced. However, the extent of such a reduction is very uncertain.

Effects on Drug Prices

The introduction of Medicaid-style rebates into the existing Part D program would create a significant incentive for drug manufacturers to alter their pricing strategies for new drugs. Of total spending in the retail pharmacy market in 2010, Medicaid accounted for about 8 percent and Part D represented about 27 percent—with purchases by low-income beneficiaries in Part D accounting for about 15 percent and purchases by other beneficiaries in Part D accounting for about 12 percent. If the share of the market receiving Medicaid-style rebates increased from 8 percent to 23 percent (with all low-income beneficiaries in Part D included), manufacturers would have an incentive to raise the launch prices (before rebates) of new brand-name drugs to mitigate the losses in revenues from the broadening of statutory rebates. However, manufacturers would not be able to offset much of the effect of broader rebates on the net prices of drugs already on the market, because the inflation rebate would apply to drugs whose before-rebate prices rose faster than general inflation. Initially, then, the prices of drugs purchased by the affected beneficiaries in Part D would probably fall to levels quite close to the current prices under Medicaid. Over time, though, manufacturers would offset much of the effect of the larger statutory rebates by launching new brand-name drugs at higher prices (before rebates), CBO anticipates. (Because the net prices to commercial buyers depend on prevailing market conditions, which would not be greatly affected by that change in Part D rules, CBO expects that manufacturers would increase the rebates offered to commercial buyers to offset much of the effect of higher before-rebate prices.) Those higher launch prices would gradually increase average drug prices for the affected beneficiaries in Part D as the pool of drugs being used changed to include more newly introduced brand-name drugs and fewer old brand-name drugs. After 15 to 20 years, CBO expects, a substantial portion of the federal savings from the statutory rebates in Part D would be offset through higher launch prices. The remaining federal savings would probably stem primarily from the inflation rebate. Over time, prices paid by certain other purchasers would rise as well. The higher launch prices for new brand-name drugs would increase the prices paid by Medicaid. Indeed, evidence shows that Medicaid's existing rebates have raised both the average prices and the lowest prices that are paid by private-sector purchasers.[65] In addition, private-sector purchasers that received the lowest prices offered by manufacturers would see an increase in some of those prices, because a larger share of the market would have access to those prices and manufacturers would therefore have an incentive to raise the prices. However, quantitative estimates of the effect on drug prices of imposing statutory rebates on purchases by low-income beneficiaries in Part D are very uncertain. It is difficult to predict what pricing strategies drug manufacturers would use and how manufacturers might set prices and rebates across their different market segments. Similarly, the response by consumers to higher drug prices is difficult to predict because it is influenced by many factors, including health conditions, drug innovations, advertising, drug coverage, and changes in medical technologies; factors that caused consumers to become less responsive to higher prices would enable drug manufacturers to raise launch prices more. The uncertainty becomes even greater for estimates that apply farther in the future, at which time the size and composition of the drug market might differ significantly from what they are today. For example, if new types of brand-name specialty drugs that treat complex or rare diseases and that tend not to have substitutes represented a larger share of the market, then manufacturers of those drugs might be able to more easily raise launch prices.[66]

Effects on the Development of New Drugs

Applying statutory rebates to drugs used by low-income beneficiaries in Part D would cause the prices paid to drug manufacturers to be much lower in the near term and somewhat lower in the long term, CBO expects. As a result, drug manufacturers would receive less income from the sale of existing drugs and lower expected profits from the development of new drugs. The reduction in prospective returns from drug development would decrease incentives to develop new drugs, particularly drugs for which a large share of users would be Medicare beneficiaries, thus making the drugs subject to the new statutory rebates.[67] In addition, the possibility that lawmakers might change the amount of the statutory rebate in the future would increase manufacturers' uncertainty about the returns that could be earned from drug development. That uncertainty would also decrease incentives to develop new drugs.

Moreover, the reduction in current revenues would mean that manufacturers would have less money from profits available to pay for research and development. Other sources of funds, such as borrowing and issuing new stock, tend to be more costly than the internal funds made available through profits.

Taken together, the decline in the expected returns from drug development, greater uncertainty about those returns, and the higher cost of funding such development would reduce the creation of new drugs compared with what it would be under current law (that is, without broader application of statutory rebates).[68] However, the extent to which drug development would decrease is very uncertain, for two main reasons. First, the extent to which manufacturers of brand-name drugs would offset the effect of a new statutory rebate with higher launch prices is uncertain. If manufacturers offset most of the effect of the statutory rebate, savings to the Part D program in the long term would be small but drug development in the long term would probably be only a little below what it would be under current law; however, if manufacturers offset less of the effect of the statutory rebate, savings to the Part D program would be larger but drug development would probably be diminished to a greater extent. Second, the magnitude of the effect on drug development of any given change in drug prices is uncertain. If that effect is small, then the impact of the statutory rebate on drug development might be modest; however, if that effect is large, then the impact of the statutory rebate on drug development might be sizable.

APPENDIX A. CALCULATING THE FEDERAL GOVERNMENT'S PAYMENTS AND BENEFICIARIES' COST-SHARING AMOUNTS FOR MEDICARE PART D

The cost of Medicare Part D is borne partly by the federal government and partly by beneficiaries of the program (see Figure A-1).

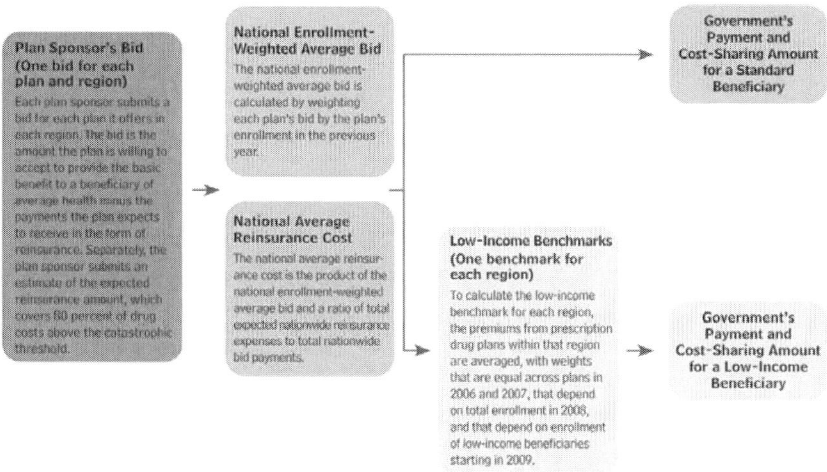

Figure A-1. (Continued).

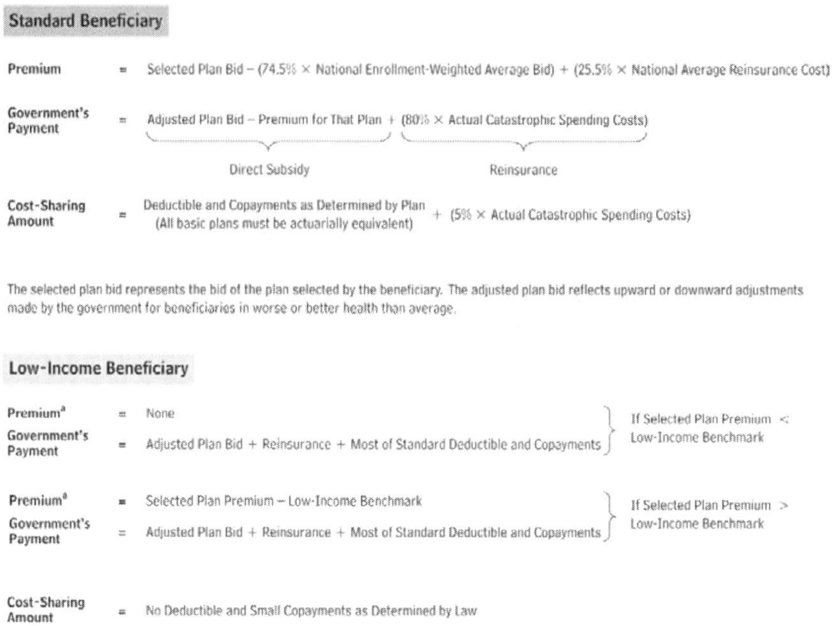

Source: Congressional Budget Office based partly on Medicare Payment Advisory Commission, *Part D Payment System* (October 2013), http://tinyurl.com/lm7sewe (PDF, 1.4 MB).

a. A small number of low-income beneficiaries are required to pay a larger premium than indicated.

Figure A-1. Calculating the Premiums, the Federal Government's Payments, and Beneficiaries' Cost-Sharing Amounts for Medicare Part D.

APPENDIX B. COMPARING THE USE AND PRICES OF DRUGS IN MEDICARE PART D AND MEDICAID FEE FOR SERVICE

The rules governing Medicare Part D and Medicaid fee for service differ in important ways that affect the rates of generic drug use and the prices of drugs consumed in the two programs. (Throughout this appendix, unless otherwise indicated, price refers to the price net of rebates.) Directly comparing the use and prices of drugs in the programs is not meaningful, however, because of differences between the programs' beneficiaries. The great majority of Medicare beneficiaries are older than 65 and were in a broad cross section of income brackets when they were younger; in contrast, most Medicaid beneficiaries are under 65 and have low income. As a result, the programs' beneficiaries exhibit a different mix of medical conditions and receive a different mix of drug therapies. On average, Medicaid beneficiaries tend to consume more-expensive drugs than do Medicare Part D beneficiaries (see Figure B-1). For example, the use of antipsychotic drugs (whose average prices are generally in the highest 25 percent of drug prices) is more prominent in Medicaid, whereas the use of cardiovascular drugs (whose average prices are generally in the lowest 25 percent of drug prices) is more common in Medicare.

To evaluate the two programs, the Congressional Budget Office (CBO) compared the use and prices of drugs consumed in Part D with an estimate of the use and prices of drugs consumed in Medicaid if Medicaid beneficiaries had exhibited the same distribution of drug use across therapeutic classes as did Part D beneficiaries. CBO did not calculate the average rate of generic drug use or prices of drugs actually observed in Medicaid for Medicaid beneficiaries.

For that comparison, CBO first identified the largest therapeutic classes. (Therapeutic classes offer a useful way to group active ingredients because the opportunities for substitution are similar for all of the drugs within a class.)

CBO chose the 53 largest classes by starting with the 30 United States pharmacopeia (USP) therapeutic classes with the greatest Part D spending and the 30 classes with the greatest number of Part D prescriptions. That procedure resulted in 41 USP therapeutic classes defined at the broadest level.[69] CBO further divided the drugs into 53 more-refined therapeutic classes, using the narrowest groupings of drugs available under the USP system within those 41 classes. Those 53 classes accounted for 73 percent of spending in the Part D program in 2010.

Second, CBO calculated the total number of days' worth of drugs supplied at the national drug code (NDC) level; each NDC corresponds to a specific active ingredient, dosage form (for example, tablet or capsule), strength (10 milligrams, for instance), package size (such as 200 pills per bottle), and manufacturer. The data on Medicaid's drug use contain the number of units dispensed for the entire year but not the number of days supplied. CBO estimated the average number of days per unit in Medicaid using claims data from Part D, assuming similar numbers of units per day (such as one 10-milligram tablet each day) for Part D and Medicaid for a given active ingredient, dosage form, and strength. Multiplying the total number of Medicaid units by the estimated days per unit produced an estimate of the number of days supplied under Medicaid. NDCs representing the same active ingredient, dosage form, and strength were grouped together using *Red Book* data. (The *Red Book* is published by Truven Health Analytics, a private firm, and includes characteristics of drugs available in the United States, such as the manufacturer's name, product name, list price, and designation as a generic or brand-name product.) The grouped NDCs were then divided into generic and brand-name drugs.

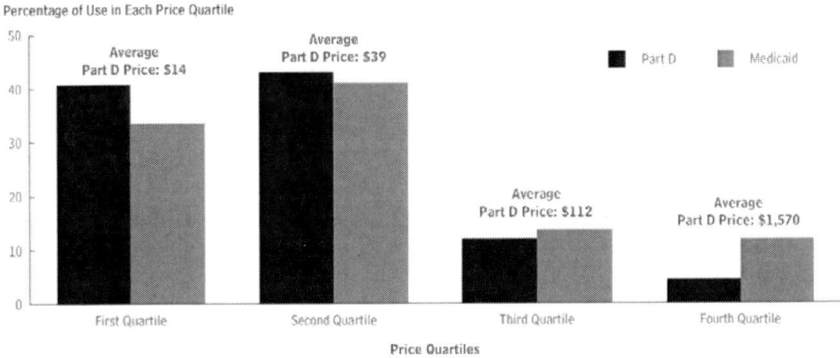

Source: Congressional Budget Office based on Medicare Part D claims data, Medicaid fee-for-service drug use data by state, and Red Book data (available from Truven Health Analytics).

Note: This figure divides the top 53 therapeutic classes, as described in Appendix B, into price quartiles based on a weighted average of the net Part D prices for brand-name and generic drugs within each therapeutic class. If, instead, Medicaid prices were used to determine which therapeutic classes go into which quartile, the pattern would be very similar. For Medicaid fee for service, the average net prices for each quartile in the figure are as follows: first quartile, $14; second quartile, $44; third quartile, $64; and fourth quartile, $750.

Figure B-1. Comparing Use of Drugs in Medicare Part D and Medicaid Fee for Service Across Price Quartiles, 2010.

The rates of generic drug use for Medicare Part D and Medicaid were calculated by determining the ratio of generic drugs to total drugs consumed for each therapeutic class in each program. To simulate the rate of generic drug use in Medicaid as if Medicaid beneficiaries had the same mix of drug use across therapeutic classes as that observed in Part D, CBO weighted each therapeutic class by the use of that class in Medicare Part D. (The rate of generic drug use in Medicare Part D was calculated the same way.) CBO repeated those calculations for the following programmatic subgroups:

Medicaid states with and without caps on the number of prescriptions dispensed per beneficiary, Medicare stand-alone plans, Medicare Advantage prescription drug plans, Part D beneficiaries who receive low-income subsidies, and Part D beneficiaries who do not qualify for those subsidies.

Thirty-one of the top 53 therapeutic classes had rates of generic drug use between 10 percent and 99 percent for either Part D or Medicaid, as reported in Table B-1. (The results for all 53 classes together are shown in the weighted averages at the bottom of the table.) This methodology captures differences in generic substitution that occur between generic and brand-name drugs with the same active ingredients as well as differences that arise as a result of substitution between different active ingredients within a therapeutic class.

For CBO's first approach to calculating the average prices of drugs, the average price for a 30-day supply within a class was calculated in a similar way as the use of generic drugs. CBO summed the prices for all of the drugs consumed in each therapeutic class for each program and then divided it by the total number of 30-day supplies for that program.[70] The average prices for Part D and Medicaid were then calculated by weighting the average prices within each class by the use of that class in Part D. The resulting average prices are what would be observed for beneficiaries following the pattern of use across therapeutic classes observed for Part D beneficiaries.

Table B-1. Rates of Generic Drug Use, by Selected Therapeutic Class, 2010

Percent

Therapeutic Class	Medicare Part D					Medicaid Fee for Service	
	Stand-Alone Plans		Medicare Advantage Plans				
	LIS	Non-LIS	LIS	Non-LIS	All Part D	States with No Caps[a]	Total (All states)
Analgesics, Combinations	99	98	99	99	98	99	99
Angiotensin II Receptor Antagonists	15	17	19	27	19	13	7
Anticoagulants	93	91	94	94	93	87	86
Anticonvulsants/GABA Augmenting	98	99	99	100	99	98	98

Table B-1. (Continued)

Percent							
Therapeutic Class	**Medicare Part D**					**Medicaid Fee for Service**	
	Stand-Alone Plans		**Medicare Advantage Plans**				
	LIS	**Non-LIS**	**LIS**	**Non-LIS**	**All Part D**	**States with No Caps[a]**	**Total (All states)**
Anticonvulsants/Mood Stabilizers	95	95	95	95	95	84	79
Antidepressants/Other	100	99	100	100	99	98	96
Antidepressants/SNRIs	96	96	97	98	97	97	95
Antidepressants/SNRIs/ Anxiolytics	62	68	68	77	67	66	61
Antipsychotics/Bipolar Agents	30	32	29	34	30	38	37
Antispasmodics/Urinary	39	38	43	53	42	49	42
Beta Blocking Agents	96	94	97	97	96	97	96
Blood Glucose Regulators	77	82	80	86	81	79	76
Bronchodilators	7	10	5	7	8	19	18
Cardiovascular Combination	58	63	61	68	63	59	52
Cholinesterase Inhibitors	9	12	11	15	11	4	4
Dyslipidemics	68	69	74	81	72	75	62
Dyslipidemics/Fibric Acids	48	54	57	67	56	46	41
Genitourinary Agents	70	69	68	71	70	50	41
Genitourinary Agents/Hormonal	56	66	61	75	66	53	41
Glucocorticoids/Inflammatory Bowel	98	97	98	98	98	94	95
Glucocorticoids/ Mineralocorticoid	90	87	91	92	90	87	83
Hormonal Agents (Thyroid)	87	68	86	77	77	90	88
Immunological Agents	66	87	73	86	79	56	56
Metabolic Bone Disease Agents	70	71	69	77	72	66	59
Nonsteroidal Anti-Inflammatories	77	75	81	83	78	85	85
Opioid Analgesics/Long Acting	62	71	68	79	67	67	62
Opioid Analgesics/Short Acting	97	99	98	99	99	82	77

Percent							
Therapeutic Class	**Medicare Part D**					**Medicaid Fee for Service**	
	Stand-Alone Plans		**Medicare Advantage Plans**				
	LIS	**Non-LIS**	**LIS**	**Non-LIS**	**All Part D**	**States with No Caps[a]**	**Total (All states)**
Proton Pump Inhibitors	64	76	74	85	73	62	41
Sleep Disorder Agents	85	88	90	94	88	85	84
Therapeutic Nutrients/Minerals	99	99	95	86	96	99	99
Vasodilators	94	94	94	94	94	94	91
Weighted Average (53 top classes)	**73**	**74**	**75**	**78**	**75**	**74**	**70**

Source: Congressional Budget Office based on Medicare Part D claims data, Medicaid fee-for-service drug use data by state, and Red Book data (available from Truven Health Analytics) to determine whether a drug was brand-name or generic.

Notes: The use rates for generic drugs are measured as days of generic drugs supplied as shares of total days of drugs supplied and then weighted across therapeutic classes based on days supplied within Medicare Part D. The number of days supplied is estimated by multiplying the units dispensed by the days supplied per unit as estimated from Part D claims data. The 31 therapeutic classes shown here had rates of generic drug use in 2010 between 10 percent and 99 percent for either Part D or Medicaid.

LIS = low-income subsidy; GABA = gamma-aminobutyric acid; SNRI = serotonin-norepinephrine reuptake inhibitor.

a. Eighteen states capped the number of prescriptions dispensed per month per beneficiary, which changed the incentive for beneficiaries to consume generic drugs within the program and thus changed the rate of generic drug use calculated for the nation as a whole.

For CBO's second approach, the agency calculated the average price for a 30-day supply of drugs by dividing each therapeutic class into groups of active ingredients. In that comparison, active ingredients that had the same dosage form and strength were grouped together. The 53 classes contain 1,347 active ingredients defined in that way, which account for 73 percent of Part D spending. The average price for each program was then calculated by weighting the average price for each active ingredient by the use of the active ingredient in Part D.

End Notes

[1] Changes made to the Part D program since its inception have increased federal spending compared with spending under the program's original design; without those changes, CBO estimates, federal spending in 2013 would have been a few percent lower. Both actual and estimated costs are net of premiums and payments from states to the federal government (often referred to as "clawback payments") that relate to the shift of beneficiaries from the Medicaid drug program to the Part D program. See Congressional Budget Office, *A Detailed Description of CBO's Cost Estimate for the Medicare Prescription Drug Benefit* (July 2004), www.cbo.gov/publication/15841.

[2] For another analysis of why the costs for Part D were lower than originally projected, see Jack Hoadley, *Medicare Part D Spending Trends: Understanding Key Drivers and the Role of Competition,* Medicare Policy Issue Brief (Henry J. Kaiser Family Foundation, May 2012), http://tinyurl.com/nfrhtt4 (PDF, 1.1 MB).

[3] See, for example, Stephen Heffler and others, "Health Spending Projections for 2002–2012," *Health Affairs* (February 7, 2003), http://dx.doi.org/10.1377/hlthaff.w3.54.

[4] CBO cites 2012 figures for two reasons. First, 2012 was the latest year for which projections of nationwide drug spending were available from CMS when CBO projected federal spending under the Medicare Modernization Act in 2003. Second, 2012 is the latest year for which data on actual nationwide drug spending, as reported by CMS in the national health expenditure accounts, are available.

[5] CBO estimated nationwide price changes using the average price for a prescription (excluding those filled by mail order). That approach did not account for any changes in the sizes of prescriptions or in the amounts of rebates over that period. To the extent that prescription sizes increased or rebates grew as a share of drug spending, the contribution of price growth to spending per person would be somewhat overstated. Average drug prices can increase either because manufacturers raise their prices or because the mix of drugs used shifts toward higher-priced drugs.

[6] See Centers for Medicare & Medicaid Services, *National Health Expenditure Projections* (published in 2004, 2006, and 2013).

[7] Differences between the growth rates of per capita drug spending in Part D and nationwide occur in part because of different patterns of drug use between the Medicare population and the U.S. population as a whole. For example, cardiovascular drugs accounted for four of the top five drug classes used by Part D beneficiaries but only two of the top five classes used nationwide. Seven cardiovascular drugs lost patent protection between 2006 and 2010; that loss contributed to the observed difference between the spending patterns of Part D beneficiaries and those of the overall population. See IMS Institute for Healthcare Informatics, *The Use of Medicines in the United States: Review of 2011* (April 2012), http://tinyurl.com/7q97mec (PDF, 1.5 MB), and *Medicare Part D at Age Five: What Has Happened to Seniors' Prescription Drug Prices?* (July 2011), http://tinyurl.com/pr5an5p (PDF, 254 KB).

[8] Prescriptions commonly provide a 30-day supply, with refills for drugs taken over a longer period.

[9] See Murray Aitken, Ernst R. Berndt, and David M. Cutler, "Prescription Drug Spending Trends in the United States: Looking Beyond the Turning Point," *Health Affairs,* vol. 28, no. 1(January–February 2009), pp. 151–160, http://dx.doi.org/ 10.1377/hlthaff.28.1.w151; and IMS Institute for Healthcare Informatics, *The Use of Medicines in the United States: Review of 2010* (April 2011), http://tinyurl.com/3p3df9e (PDF, 1.8 MB).

[10] Although the market share of new generic drugs (as measured by quantity used) increased by 12 percentage points nationwide from 2007 to 2010, the market share of the corresponding brand-name drugs that lost patent protection between 2006 and 2010 declined by only 8 percentage points. That difference probably arose from the substitution of drugs that are

therapeutically similar and from other factors that increased the market share of drugs losing patent protection relative to the market share of other drugs that did not recently lose patent protection.

[11] The weights represent the number of days supplied for brand-name and generic drugs.

[12] That calculation reflects simplifying assumptions that the market share of drugs (as measured by quantity used) would have been unaffected by that difference in price and that the prices of drugs that recently lost patent protection would have risen at the same rate as prices of patent-protected brand-name drugs (8.5 percent annually, on average) rather than declining by 19.8 percent annually, on average. The 1.2 percent increase in the average retail price of drugs shown in Table1-2 differs from the 0.5 percent decrease in the average price of a 30-day supply of drugs shown in Table1-1 because Table1-2 does not include the effects of rebates or the substitution of drugs that are therapeutically similar, both of which are accounted for in Table1-1.

[13] See Congressional Budget Office, *Effects of Using Generic Drugs on Medicare's Prescription Drug Spending* (September 2010), www.cbo.gov/publication/21800.

[14] See Food and Drug Administration, *2013 Novel New Drug Summary* (January 2014), http://tinyurl.com/llgqn9o (PDF, 3 MB).

[15] See Henry G. Grabowski and John M. Vernon, "Returns to R&D on New Drug Introductions in the 1980s," *Journal of Health Economics,* vol. 13 (1994), pp. 383–406, http://tinyurl.com/d7betra; and Henry Grabowski, John Vernon, and Joseph A. DiMasi, "Returns on Research and Development for 1990s New Drug Introductions," *Pharmaco Economics,* vol. 20, no. 3 (March 2002), pp. 11–29, www.ncbi.nlm.nih.gov/ pubmed/ 12457422.

[16] See IMS Institute for Healthcare Informatics, *The Use of Medicines in the United States: Review of 2011* (April 2012), http://tinyurl.com/7q97mec (PDF, 1.5 MB).

[17] See Murray Aitken, Ernst R. Berndt, and David M. Cutler, "Prescription Drug Spending Trends in the United States: Looking Beyond the Turning Point," *Health Affairs,* vol. 28, no. 1(January–February 2009), pp. 151–160, http://dx.doi.org/ 10.1377/hlthaff.28.1.w151. Price refers to a weighted average of the prices of the brand-name version of a drug and its generic counterparts.

[18] See Congressional Budget Office, *Offsetting Effects of Prescription Drug Use on Medicare's Spending for Medical Services* (November 2012), www.cbo.gov/publication/43741.

[19] See IMS Institute for Healthcare Informatics, *The Use of Medicines in the United States: Review of 2010* (April 2011), http://tinyurl.com/3p3df9e (PDF, 1.8 MB).

[20] See IMS Institute for Healthcare Informatics, *The Use of Medicines in the United States: Review of 2011* (April 2012), http://tinyurl.com/7q97mec (PDF, 1.5 MB).

[21] See Congressional Budget Office, *A Detailed Description of CBO's Cost Estimate for the Medicare Prescription Drug Benefit* (July 2004), pp. 3–5, www.cbo.gov/publication/15841.

[22] See Medicare Payment Advisory Commission, *Report to the Congress: Medicare Payment Policy* (March 2012), p. 345, http://tinyurl.com/oetakc3 (PDF, 9 MB); that report suggests that 10 percent of Medicare enrollees lack drug coverage or have coverage that is less extensive than that available through Part D and that those enrollees incur drug spending that is below average.

[23] For example, see James J. Choi and others, "For Better or for Worse: Default Effects and 401(k) Savings Behavior," in David A. Wise, ed., *Perspectives on the Economics of Aging* (University of Chicago Press, 2004), www.nber.org/chapters/c10341.

[24] Medicare beneficiaries generally cannot avoid enrolling in Part A.

[25] For research supporting the conclusion that excessive choice reduces consumers' responsiveness, see, for example, Sheena Sethi-Iyengar, Gur Huberman, and Wei Jiang, "How Much Choice Is Too Much? Contributions for 401(k) Retirement Plans," Chapter 5 in Olivia S. Mitchell and Stephen P. Utkus, eds., *Pension Design and Structure: New Lessons from Behavioral Finance* (Oxford University Press, September 2004), http://tinyurl.com/ n2uu597 (PDF, 25 MB). For research suggesting that an abundance of choices does not

significantly influence consumers' behavior, see, for example, Benjamin Scheibehenne, Raner Greifeneder, and Peter M. Todd, "Can There Ever Be Too Many Options? A Meta-Analytic Review of Choice Overload," *Journal of Consumer Research*, vol. 37, no. 3 (October 2010), pp. 409–425, http://dx.doi.org/10.1086/651235.

[26] For more information on drug spending and on the structure of Part D, see Congressional Budget Office, *Spending Patterns for Prescription Drugs Under Medicare Part D* (December 2011), www.cbo.gov/publication/42692.

[27] Enrollees in stand-alone plans represented about 65 percent of Part D enrollment during the 2007–2010 period covered by this analysis. Almost 80 percent of those enrollees joined a basic plan, with the remaining 20 percent in enhanced plans. Excluding enrollees who received low-income subsidies, about 60 percent of enrollees in stand-alone plans selected a basic plan.

[28] Other researchers have analyzed the effects of competition between Medicare Advantage plans and found that bids tended to be lower when a larger number of plan sponsors were present. See Zirui Song, Mary Beth Landrum, and Michael E. Chernew, "Competitive Bidding in Medicare Advantage: Who Benefits From Competition," *American Journal of Managed Care,* vol. 18, no. 9 (September 2012), pp. 546—552, www.ncbi.nlm.nih.gov/ pmc/articles/ PMC3519284.

[29] For evidence that beneficiaries favor plans with lower premiums and for more information on plan choice, see Jason Abaluck and Jonathan Gruber, "Choice Inconsistencies Among the Elderly: Evidence From Plan Choice in the Medicare Part D Program," *American Economic Review,* vol. 101, no. 4 (June 2011), pp. 1180–1210, http://dx.doi.org/10.1257/ aer.101.4.1180; and Jonathan D. Ketcham, Nicolai V. Kuminoff, and Christopher A. Powers, *Choice Inconsistencies Among the Elderly: Evidence From Plan Choice in the Medicare Part D Program: Comment,* Working Paper 52 (RWJF Scholars in Health Policy Research Program, August 2013), http://tinyurl.com/ksdowsh (PDF, 719 KB).

[30] In 2007, the average premium among plans chosen by enrollees was $27. That number is lower than the average monthly premium offered in the 34 Part D bidding regions ($36) because enrollees tended to choose less expensive plans.

[31] Other researchers have also found that beneficiaries who switch plans lower their premiums and out-of-pocket costs. For example, see Jonathan D. Ketcham and others, "Sinking, Swimming, or Learning to Swim in Medicare Part D," *American Economic Review*, vol. 102, no. 6 (October 2012), pp. 2639–2673, http://dx.doi.org/10.1257/aer.102.6.2639.

[32] Each plan sponsor may offer more than one plan. CBO's analysis measures competition by the number of plan sponsors rather than plans, because it is plan sponsors that determine the pricing and other characteristics of the plans. In CBO's view, plan sponsors can generally predict how many competitors they will face in the coming year as they prepare their bids. That view is consistent with the approach used in other analyses; see, for example, Dennis P. Scanlon and others, "Competition in Health Insurance Markets: Limitations of Current Measures for Policy Analysis," *Medical Care Research and Review,* vol. 63, no. 6 (December 2006), pp. 37S–55S, www.ncbi.nlm.nih.gov/pubmed/17099129.

[33] For more information, see Andrew Stocking and others, *Examining the Number of Competitors and the Cost of Medicare PartD*, Working Paper 2014-04 (Congressional Budget Office, July 2014), www.cbo.gov/publication/45553.

[34] Those estimated savings reflect only changes in the bids of basic plans with a premium above the low-income benchmark in the previous year. (Enrollees in such plans account for about 20 percent of total Part D enrollment between 2007 and 2010.) Reductions in the number of competitors may also be associated with increases in the bids of other types of plans—such as enhanced plans or Medicare Advantage plans—but those changes have not been analyzed here and thus are not included in the estimate.

[35] The additional information could be personalized for each beneficiary on the basis of his or her prior drug use. See, for example, Jeffrey R. Kling and others, "Comparison Friction:

Experimental Evidence From Medicare Drug Plans," *Quarterly Journal of Economics*, vol. 127, no. 1 (February 2012), pp. 199–235, http://dx.doi.org/10.1093/qje/qjr055.

[36] By contrast, low-income beneficiaries who have actively chosen their current plan are not reassigned by CMS if their plan's premium exceeds the benchmark; instead, they are charged the difference in cost between the benchmark and their plan's premium.

[37] A rule that has been in force since 2011 (and was also in force in 2007 and 2008) reduces the cost to plans if their premium exceeds the benchmark. Plans with a monthly premium that exceeds the benchmark by no more than a specified amount ($2 in 2007, $1 in 2008, and $2 in 2011 and subsequent years) can reduce their premium for low-income beneficiaries to the benchmark. For plans that choose that option, no new low-income beneficiaries will be automatically assigned to them for that year, but they will not lose the low-income beneficiaries who have already enrolled.

[38] Because lower-cost plans could have more restrictive formularies, an alternative to that design would be to have the government preferentially assign low-income beneficiaries to plans that had a similar formulary and premiums in the lowest 25 percent of the distribution in a region. Determining whether formularies are "similar" could be challenging, however.

[39] Plans have an incentive not to overestimate spending because that would cause their premiums to rise and thus reduce enrollment.

[40] See Henry J. Kaiser Family Foundation, *Policy Options to Sustain Medicare for the Future* (January 2013), http://tinyurl.com/ lsqwvqc (PDF, 13 MB).

[41] The thresholds of drug spending relative to anticipated spending that trigger risk corridor payments were doubled in 2008. For more on risk corridors, see Congressional Budget Office, *A Detailed Description of CBO's Cost Estimate for the Medicare Prescription Drug Benefit* (July 2004), pp. 35–37, www.cbo.gov/ publication/15841.

[42] See John Hsu and others, "Distributing $800 Billion: An Early Assessment of Medicare Part D Risk Adjustment," *Health Affairs*, vol. 28, no. 1 (January 2009), pp. 215–225, http://dx.doi.org/10.1377/hlthaff.28.1.215.

[43] For an analysis of the new method, see John Kautter and others, "Improvements in Medicare Part D Risk Adjustment: Beneficiary Access and Payment Accuracy," *Medical Care*, vol. 50, no. 12 (December 2012), pp. 1102–1108, http://tinyurl.com/c985szf. For an analysis of the prior method, see John Hsu and others, "Distributing $800 Billion: An Early Assessment of Medicare Part D Risk Adjustment," *Health Affairs,* vol. 28, no. 1 (January 2009), pp. 215–225, http://dx.doi.org/10.1377/hlthaff.28.1.215. For further discussion of why risk adjustment is important in a Medicare drug benefit, see Congressional Budget Office, *Issues in Designing a Prescription Drug Benefit for Medicare* (October 2002), pp. 22–23, www.cbo.gov/publication/14182.

[44] That finding reflects the assumption that only basic plans with a premium above the low-income benchmark raised their bids in response to lower numbers of plan sponsors. To the extent that plans with a premium below the low-income benchmark or enhanced plans also raised their bids in response to lower numbers of plan sponsors, the reduction in plan sponsors could explain more of the increase in administrative costs and profits per beneficiary between 2007 and 2010.

[45] The remaining 10 percent was provided by private managed care organizations. Those organizations are not included in this analysis because data about their costs and generic drug use were not available when the analysis was completed.

[46] Some states also negotiate supplemental rebates. Such rebates were equal to about 4 percent of Medicaid's total payments to retail pharmacies for brand-name drugs in 2010. Because supplemental rebates are small relative to statutory rebates (which were equal to about 54 percent of Medicaid's total payments to retail pharmacies for brand-name drugs in 2010) and because data on supplemental rebates are not available by drug, CBO did not include them in the quantitative analyses presented in this section .

[47] The use of specialty tiers with higher copayments could also serve as a mechanism for plan sponsors to discourage some beneficiaries from joining their plans, particularly

beneficiaries who need expensive drugs and thus probably cost more to insure. To keep plans from discouraging expensive beneficiaries from enrolling, the government's payment to each plan is adjusted for each beneficiary's expected cost—a process known as risk adjustment (described in Section 2).

[48] See Mark Duggan and Fiona Scott Morton, "The Effect of Medicare Part D on Pharmaceutical Prices and Utilization," *American Economic Review,* vol. 100, no. 1 (March 2010), pp. 590–607, http://dx.doi.org/10.1257/aer.100.1.590, and "The Medium-Term Impact of Medicare Part D on Pharmaceutical Prices," *American Economic Review,* vol. 101, no. 3 (May 2011), pp. 387–392, http://dx.doi.org/10.1257/aer.101.3.387.

[49] In some cases, manufacturers might also pay a rebate to have their drug included in a plan's formulary, even if it is not on the preferred tier.

[50] The six designated classes are anticonvulsants, antidepressants, antineoplastics, antipsychotics, anti retrovirals, and immuno-suppressants.

[51] See Department of Health and Human Services, Office of Inspector General, *Concerns With Rebates in the Medicare Part D Program,* OEI-02-08-00050 (March 2011), www.oig.hhs.gov/oei/ reports/oei-02-08-00050.pdf (764 KB), which reports that "five [of the six evaluated] sponsors received higher formulary rebates for beneficiaries eligible for the low-income subsidy than for other Part D beneficiaries" (p. 15).

[52] Medicaid also requires manufacturers to pay a rebate on their generic drugs equal to 13.1 percent of the average manufacturer's price.

[53] Pharmacy benefit managers often administer drug benefits and negotiate for rebates from brand-name drug manufacturers on behalf of drug plans in the private sector, including those offered by Part D and those offered to people younger than 65. Excluding pharmacy benefit managers as qualified purchasers when those purchases are made at a community pharmacy removes roughly 80 percent of retail drug spending from the best-price calculation. However, mail-order purchases handled by pharmacy benefit managers are included in the best-price calculation. For more information about the role of pharmacy benefit managers, see Federal Trade Commission, *Pharmacy Benefit Managers: Ownership of Mail-Order Pharmacies* (August 2005), http://tinyurl.com/ pbnf24z.

[54] The four states that imposed caps on the number of brand-name prescriptions were Alabama, Illinois, Kansas, and Maine.

[55] Thirteen states imposed caps on the total number of prescriptions per beneficiary: Arkansas, California, Georgia, Kentucky, Louisiana, Mississippi, North Carolina, Oklahoma, South Carolina, Tennessee, Texas, Utah, and West Virginia. In addition, New York placed caps on the number of prescriptions dispensed to a beneficiary that vary depending on his or her health conditions. For more detailed information on the limits that states place on Medicaid prescriptions, see Henry J. Kaiser Family Foundation, "Medicaid Benefits: Prescription Drugs" (accessed September 30, 2013), http://tinyurl.com/lgx8yza.

[56] The price of drugs, as used in this section of the report, represents the average price (net of rebates) of brand-name drugs and generic drugs, weighted by the use of each type of drug and with drugs grouped by therapeutic class or active ingredient.

[57] Within Medicaid, states that did not impose caps on prescriptions had a higher rate of generic drug use than the program as a whole (see Table 3-1). Considering only states without caps, CBO estimated that the average price of drugs within Part D would have been 10 percent higher if the mix of drugs used within therapeutic classes matched that of Medicaid rather than that of Part D; conversely, the average price of drugs within Medicaid would have been 12 percent lower if the mix of drugs within therapeutic classes matched that of Part D rather than that of Medicaid. Thus, some of the difference between Part D's and Medicaid's use of lower-priced drugs within therapeutic classes occurred because ofthe lower rate of generic drug use in states that placed caps on prescriptions that could be filled within the Medicaid program.

[58] Across both programs, CBO calculated prices net of rebates on brand-name and generic drugs. (Rebates on generic drugs tend to be very small.) Rebate data are not available to calculate

separate estimates of prices for the Part D subgroups shown in Table3-1 (such as Medicare Advantage prescription drug plans and standalone plans).

59 States that did not cap prescriptions had a higher rate of generic drug use than Medicaid as a whole (see Table 3-1). Considering only states without caps, CBO estimated that the average price of a 30-day drug supply in Medicaid would have been $35.

60 CBO's estimate based on weights for active ingredients credits both Part D and Medicaid for using generic versions of the same active ingredients but does not credit them for using less expensive drugs with different active ingredients within the same therapeutic classes.

61 With that approach, the average price is roughly the same for states without caps on prescriptions as it is for all of Medicaid.

62 Expanding that analysis to all active ingredients (not just those in the top 53 classes), CBO estimated that the average price of a 30-day supply in 2010 was $35 in Medicaid and $54 in Part D. CBO could not make a comparable estimate for all classes weighted by the use of drugs in each class because of concerns about the accuracy of converting dosage measures of active ingredients to 30-day supplies for smaller therapeutic classes.

63 For more information, see Congressional Budget Office, letter tothe Honorable Paul Ryan about the effect of the March health legislation on prescription drug prices (November 4, 2010), www.cbo.gov/publication/21639.

64 See "Health—Option 11" in Congressional Budget Office, *Options for Reducing the Deficit: 2014 to 2023* (November 2013), pp. 234–235, www.cbo.gov/budget-options/2013/44687. For examples of similar legislative proposals, see S. 740 and H.R. 1588, both titled the Medicare Drug Savings Act of 2013. In those proposals, plan sponsors would still receive whatever rebates they negotiated with the manufacturers, but any difference between the statutory rebate and their negotiated rebates would be paid to the federal government. Estimated budgetary savings from those proposals and others could differ greatly from the estimate described here depending on the details of the proposals.

65 See Mark Duggan and Fiona M. Scott Morton, "The Distortion-ary Effects of Government Procurement: Evidence From Medicaid Prescription Drug Purchasing," *Quarterly Journal of Economics,* vol. 121, no. 1 (February 2006), pp. 1–30, http://dx.doi.org/ 10.1093/ qje/121.1.1; and Congressional Budget Office, *How the Medicaid Rebate on Prescription Drugs Affects Pricing in the Pharmaceutical Industry* (January 1996), www.cbo.gov/ publication/ 14944.

66 The effects discussed in this section would generally be more substantial if Medicaid-style rebates were applied to all drug purchases within Part D, not just those by low-income beneficiaries, because the scope of drug purchases that would be affected by the policy would be much larger.

67 The U.S. drug market represents about one-third of global sales, so changes in revenues from the U.S. market can significantly affect the total revenues of drug manufacturers. For information on how drug prices and market size affect research and development, see Oliver de Mouzon and others, *Market Size and Pharmaceutical Innovation,* Discussion Paper Series No. 8367 (Center for Economic Policy Research, April 2011), www.cepr.org/pubs/ dps/ DP8367.asp; and Carmelo Giaccotto, Rexford E. Santerre, and John A. Vernon, "Drug Prices and Research and Development Investment Behavior in the Pharmaceutical Industry," *Journal of Law and Economics*, vol. 48, no. 1 (April 2005), pp. 195–214, www.jstor.org/stable/10.1086/426882.

68 For discussion of the implications of research and development for the introduction of new drugs, see Congressional Budget Office, *Research and Development in the Pharmaceutical Industry* (October 2006), www.cbo.gov/publication/18176.

69 That level is defined by the combination of USP therapeutic categories and pharmacologic classes. See U.S. Pharmacopeial Convention, "USP Medicare Model Guidelines," http://tinyurl.com/mzqhe45.

[70] Some states negotiate for rebates beyond the statutory rebate; those supplemental rebates, which average 4 percent of Medicaid's retail spending on brand-name drugs, are not included in this analysis because data on the size of those rebates are not available by drug.

In: Medicare's Prescription Drug Program ISBN: 978-1-63463-122-8
Editor: Gloria R. Pattinson

Chapter 2

EFFECTS OF USING GENERIC DRUGS ON MEDICARE'S PRESCRIPTION DRUG SPENDING*

Julie Somers

SUMMARY

In 2006, Medicare began offering outpatient prescription drug benefits to senior citizens and people with disabilities in a program called Part D. Unlike other Medicare benefits covered under the traditional fee-for-service program—in which providers are paid an administratively determined price for each covered service (or bundle of services) they provide—prices in Part D are not set by the government. Instead, private plans deliver the drug benefit and negotiate their own drug prices while competing with each other for enrollees.

That framework was intended to provide those plans with incentives to make their drug benefits attractive to potential enrollees and to control their costs. One important way in which they do so is by negotiating with manufacturers of brand-name drugs for rebates. Another important mechanism is managing enrollees' use of prescription drugs—and in particular, encouraging the use of generic drugs. Using differences in copayments and other methods, plans can encourage enrollees to switch from brand-name drugs to their less expensive generic equivalents—a

* This is an edited, reformatted and augmented version of a report issued by the Congressional Budget Office, September 2010.

practice known as generic substitution. Plans can also encourage enrollees to switch from a brand-name drug to the generic form of a different drug that is in the same therapeutic class, which is one form of a practice known as therapeutic substitution. (Therapeutic substitution can also include switching from a higher priced brand-name drug to a lower priced brand-name drug in the same class.)

The Congressional Budget Office (CBO) used data from the Centers for Medicare and Medicaid Services on prescriptions filled in 2007 under Part D to assess how successful plans have been in encouraging the use of generic drugs and how much additional savings could arise from the wider use of such drugs. Developing policy tools to achieve additional savings from greater use of generic drugs is a further challenge not addressed in this study.

Potential Savings from Generic Substitution

In 2007, total payments to plans and pharmacies from the Part D program and its enrollees were about $60 billion. The total number of prescriptions filled under Part D was about 1 billion, of which 65 percent were filled with generic drugs, 5 percent were filled with multiple-source brand-name drugs (brand-name drugs that are also available in generic versions), and 30 percent were filled with single-source brand-name drugs (brand-name drugs for which no chemically equivalent generic versions are available). Even though a majority of prescriptions were filled with generic drugs, their lower prices meant that those prescriptions accounted for only 25 percent of total prescription drug costs.

Using the Part D data, CBO estimates that dispensing generic drugs rather than their brand-name counterparts reduced total prescription drug costs in 2007 by about $33 billion. Thus, total payments to plans and pharmacies from the Part D program and its enrollees would have been about $93 billion—or 55 percent higher—if no generics had been available. That analysis holds several factors constant and reflects CBO's assessment (discussed below) that generic entry is unlikely to have a substantial effect on either the price of the brand-name drug or the total quantity (including brand-name and generic versions) of the drug sold.

The savings from using generic drugs accrued to Medicare and its enrollees. In 2007, Medicare made 72 percent of the total payments to plans and pharmacies under Part D, and enrollees paid for the remainder through premiums, deductibles, coinsurance, and copayments. A reasonable judgment is that those shares of payments would also apply to the savings from generic utilization—which translates into savings of about $24 billion for the Part D program in 2007 and about $9 billion for its enrollees. The actual share of savings going to each group could have been somewhat higher or lower, however, depending on a number of factors, such as how the savings altered spending across the various coverage phases of the Part D program.

CBO also analyzed the potential for additional savings from increased generic substitution and found that it is comparatively small. If all of the 45 million prescriptions filled with multiple-source brand-name drugs had instead been filled with their generic counterparts, an additional $900 million—representing less than 2 percent of total payments to plans and pharmacies from the Part D program and its enrollees in 2007—would have been saved. Using their shares of payments to plans and pharmacies to allocate those savings, the Part D program would have saved about $650 million, and its enrollees would have saved about $250 million.

Potential Savings from Therapeutic Substitution

Single-source brand-name drugs accounted for 68 percent of total prescription drug costs under Part D in 2007, even though those drugs accounted for only about 30 percent of prescriptions. Plans could have achieved some savings from that group of drugs by encouraging enrollees to switch to the generic form of a different drug in the same therapeutic class—that is, a drug designed to treat the same medical condition.

The potential to reduce costs by promoting such therapeutic substitution depends on the number of single-source prescriptions that it would be medically appropriate to switch. To assess the potential for such savings, CBO examined potential therapeutic substitution for seven therapeutic classes identified by the Medicare program as providing opportunities for such substitution. If all of the single-source brand-name prescriptions in those seven classes had been switched to generic drugs from the same class, prescription drug costs would have been reduced by $4 billion in 2007, or 7 percent of total payments to plans and pharmacies in that year. Again using their overall shares of payments to plans and pharmacies to allocate those savings, Medicare spending would have been reduced by $2.9 billion, and enrollees' spending would have been reduced by $1.1 billion. As with generic substitution, the actual share of the savings going to either group could have been somewhat higher or lower.

The potential savings from therapeutic substitution to generic drugs could have been higher or lower than those estimates, for two reasons. On the one hand, the reduction in costs in the seven therapeutic classes that feasibly could have been achieved would be less than $4 billion because in many cases it would have been medically inappropriate to switch a prescription from a single-source brand-name drug to the generic form of a therapeutically similar drug. Some drugs in a class either may be more effective than others for some of the population or may not be safe for people with other health conditions. Consequently, a pharmacist must obtain the consent of the prescribing physician before substituting a generic drug for a single-source drug that is in the same therapeutic class but is not chemically equivalent.

On the other hand, savings from therapeutic substitution to generic drugs could have been much higher than $4billion to the extent that other classes of drugs also would have presented options for substitution. The seven classes that CBO evaluated represented only about one-fifth of total prescription drug costs and 15 percent of the cost of single-source brand-name drugs under Part D. Even if the share of drugs that feasibly could have been switched in those other classes had been lower than in the classes that Medicare highlighted, those switches would generate additional savings. Compared with the potential for additional savings from generic substitution, the potential for additional savings from therapeutic substitution was greater both because the savings per prescription were greater (given the relative prices of the specific drugs involved) and because slightly more prescriptions had the potential to be switched.

Policymakers would face several challenges in developing tools to achieve any additional savings from the expanded use of generic drugs—particularly in the case of therapeutic substitution. About half of Part D spending is on behalf of enrollees who have lower incomes and thus qualify for additional subsidies. Policies that used financial incentives to steer enrollees toward certain drugs might not be effective for that population because Medicare pays nearly all of their costs. In addition, plans must meet certain requirements intended to ensure that enrollees have access to the drugs that they need and to prevent the plans from discouraging beneficiaries with high drug costs from enrolling; those requirements limit plans' ability to steer drug use. Finally, it could be difficult for policymakers to design policies so that switches from single-source brand-name drugs to generic drugs were made only when medically appropriate.

Implications of Future Developments

The estimates of actual savings from generic substitution in 2007 and potential savings that could have been realized from greater generic and therapeutic substitution during that year illustrate that using generic drugs in the future can reduce spending under Part D. However, the potential for such savings will vary from year to year depending on many factors, including the extent to which generic drugs and new brand-name drugs enter the market.

Over the next several years, entities that pay for prescription drugs will benefit from a wave of brand-name drugs in high-priced therapeutic classes losing patent protection or other periods of exclusivity, which will allow generic drugs to enter those markets for the first time. Also, relatively few new brand-name drug products are expected to reach the market in the near term. If the current rate of generic substitution is maintained, first-time generic entry occurring through 2012 will generate about $14 billion in additional savings from generic substitution, in addition to the $33 billion in savings calculated above (where both figures apply to 2007 spending patterns). However, potential savings from therapeutic substitution for the classes that CBO considered would be reduced from $4 billion to about $2 billion (also based on 2007 spending). That reduction occurs because some of the prescriptions that would have been shifted to a different generic drug (when generating the estimate for therapeutic substitution in 2007) will have their own generic competitor by 2012; those savings are thus included in the $14 billion figure for additional savings from generic substitution.

Two other important considerations stem from the provisions of the recently enacted legislation on health care (the Patient Protection and Affordable Care Act, as modified by the Health and Education Reconciliation Act of 2010). First and foremost, the coverage gap in the Part D benefit—a range of spending in which many enrollees have to pay all of their drug costs—will gradually be closed. As a result, the total amount of drug spending under Part D, the mix of generic and brand-name drugs used, and the federal government's share of drug spending will all change at least to some degree. In addition, the legislation created a regulatory pathway for approving drugs that are "biosimilar" to brand-name biologic products—drugs that are made from living organisms and that tend to be very expensive. How quickly those biosimilar drugs are developed and used, how they are priced, and whether they will be treated under regulation in the same manner as generic drugs for purposes of closing the coverage gap under Part D will all have important implications for future prescription drug spending.

In 2006, Medicare began offering outpatient prescription drug benefits to senior citizens and people with disabilities through the Medicare Prescription Drug Benefit Program (Part D). The program relies upon private plans to deliver those benefits to its enrollees. In contrast to the traditional fee-for-service programs employed to deliver other Medicare benefits—in which providers of health care are paid an administratively determined price for each covered service, or bundle of services, that enrollees receive—prices in Part D are negotiated by private plans that compete with one another for enrollees. That framework was intended to give plans incentives to make their drug benefits attractive to potential enrollees and to control costs. Toward that end, plans use various techniques to manage enrollees' use of drugs and to negotiate price rebates from drug manufacturers and discounts from pharmacies.

Generic substitution, the practice of switching a prescription from a brand-name drug to a less expensive chemically equivalent generic drug, is one prominent approach to controlling costs.[1] This analysis uses data provided by the Centers for Medicare and Medicaid Services (CMS) on prescriptions filled under Part D in 2007 to assess the extent to which generic substitution reduced prescription drug spending in that year. The study also provides estimates of how much more spending could have been reduced in 2007 by additional generic substitution and by one form of another practice—known as therapeutic substitution—in which a prescription is switched from a brand-name drug to the generic form of a different drug that is in the same therapeutic class. In addition, the outlook for future savings from using generic drugs is briefly discussed. To explain who benefits from lower prescription drug spending and the incentives of enrollees and private plans to control such spending, the study begins by describing the design of the Part D benefit, the distribution of spending under Part D, and the role of private plans in the Part D program.

Overview of the Medicare Prescription Drug Benefit Program

Medicare Part D has about 28 million enrollees, and the Congressional Budget Office (CBO) estimates that net outlays will amount to $48 billion in fiscal year 2010.[2] The program as it existed during its first five years is described below, with a particular focus on 2007 because this study uses detailed data from that year. The health care legislation enacted in March 2010 makes changes to Part D that will be phased in over a 10-year period.[3] The changes expected in 2011 and beyond from that legislation are also described.

Design of the Medicare Prescription Drug Benefit

The Medicare prescription drug benefit is delivered by private plans. Private prescription drug plans—sometimes called "stand-alone" drug plans—offer only prescription drug coverage and are designed for enrollees who get their other Medicare benefits in the traditional fee-for-service program. In addition, private health plans, called Medicare Advantage plans, offer prescription drug coverage that is integrated with the health care coverage they provide to Medicare beneficiaries under Part C.[4]

Original Benefit Design. Before the recent enactment of health care legislation, the Part D standard prescription drug benefit included these phases of coverage:

- deductible paid by the beneficiary ($265 in 2007);
- Coverage paid by the plan for 75 percent of drug costs between the deductible and the initial coverage limit ($2,400 in 2007);
- A coverage gap beyond the initial coverage limit in which no further coverage is provided until an enrollee has incurred out-of-pocket drug costs for the year exceeding the catastrophic threshold ($3,850 in 2007, which corresponds to about $5,450 in total drug spending for someone who has no supplemental drug coverage); and
- Coverage of about 95 percent of drug costs beyond that threshold, with 15 percent of those costs paid by the plan and 80 percent paid by the Part D program. That coverage is not capped.

Over time, the dollar values that set those thresholds are indexed to growth in drug spending per enrollee, so that the benefit covers roughly the same share of drug costs from year to year.

Plans may offer the standard benefit established in law, alternative prescription drug benefits that are actuarially equivalent to the standard prescription drug benefit, or benefits that are enhanced in some way. The standard benefit establishes the minimal level of coverage within Part D, but most people receive benefits that have different cost-sharing requirements—such as having a copayment that is a fixed dollar amount per prescription rather than a percentage of the prescription's cost. To be actuarially equivalent, an alternative benefit design must cover the same share of enrollees' drug costs, on average, as the standard benefit. Enhanced plans have a higher actuarial value.

For enrollees in stand-alone plans in 2007, about 20 percent were in standard benefit plans, 60 percent were in actuarially equivalent plans, and 20 percent were in enhanced benefit plans. By 2009, about 10 percent of enrollees in stand-alone plans were in standard benefit plans, 64 percent were in actuarially equivalent plans, and 26 percent were in enhanced benefit plans. Enrollees in Medicare Advantage plans were predominantly in enhanced benefit plans (80 percent in 2007 and 94 percent in 2009). Only about 1 percent of enrollees in Medicare Advantage plans were in standard benefit plans over that time period.[5]

For each enrollee, Medicare provides plans with a subsidy of about 75 percent of the average cost of the standard prescription drug benefit. (A portion of that subsidy is provided by paying 80 percent of drug costs above the catastrophic threshold, and the rest is made as a per-enrollee payment.) Most enrollees pay for the rest of the benefit and any enhanced benefits through premiums. Enrollees who have low income and few assets, however, may qualify for additional subsidies. For those enrollees, Medicare pays for nearly all of the premiums, deductibles, coinsurance, and copayments and for drug spending in the coverage gap.[6]

Medicare also subsidizes prescription drug plans provided by employers and unions for their retirees. To qualify for that subsidy (called the retiree drug subsidy), the plans must offer benefits that are at least actuarially equivalent to the standard prescription drug benefit under Part D. As long as they meet those requirements, the plan sponsors have complete flexibility over the design of the benefits they provide.

Recently Enacted Changes. The recently enacted health care legislation makes several changes affecting the coverage gap in Part D. Beginning in 2011, manufacturers will be required to provide a 50 percent discount off the negotiated price of brand-name drugs included in a plan's formulary—a list of drugs that the plan will pay for—to an enrollee when his or her prescription drug spending is in the coverage gap. Those manufacturers' discounts will be counted toward enrollees' out-of-pocket costs for determining whether they have reached the catastrophic threshold. Enrollees who receive low-income subsidies or are in plans receiving the retiree drug subsidy will not be eligible for the discount (presumably because they would not have faced the coverage gap under prior law).

In addition, and also starting in 2011, plans will provide an increasing amount of coverage under the standard prescription drug benefit for drugs purchased in the range of spending that would have constituted the coverage gap; plans that provide an actuarially equivalent benefit will have to increase their value correspondingly. For brand-name drugs purchased in that spending range, plans will pay 2.5 percent of their cost in 2013, increasing to 25percent by 2020 and beyond. For generic drugs purchased in that spending range, plans will pay 7 percent of the cost in 2011; that coverage will increase each year to reach a total of 75 percent by 2020, where it will remain (see Table 1). As a result, by 2020, enrollees will pay 25percent of drug costs in the former coverage gap, just as they do in the initial phase of coverage.

Table 1. Cost Sharing and Manufacturers' Discounts for Prescription Drugs in the Former Medicare Part D Coverage Gap (Percentage of prescription drug spending)

	Brand-Name Drugs			Generic Drugs		
	Enrollees' Cost Sharing	Plans' Cost Sharing	Manufacturers' Discounts	Enrollees' Cost Sharing	Plans' Cost Sharing	Manufacturers' Discounts
2010	100.0	n.a.	n.a.	100.0	n.a.	n.a.
2011	50.0	n.a.	50.0	93.0	7.0	n.a.
2012	50.0	n.a.	50.0	86.0	14.0	n.a.
2013	47.5	2.5	50.0	79.0	21.0	n.a.
2014	47.5	2.5	50.0	72.0	28.0	n.a.
2015	45.0	5.0	50.0	65.0	35.0	n.a.
2016	45.0	5.0	50.0	58.0	42.0	n.a.
2017	40.0	10.0	50.0	51.0	49.0	n.a.
2018	35.0	15.0	50.0	44.0	56.0	n.a.
2019	30.0	20.0	50.0	37.0	63.0	n.a.
2020 and Beyond	25.0	25.0	50.0	25.0	75.0	n.a.

Source: Congressional Budget Office based on the provisions of the Patient Protection and Affordable Care Act (Public Law 111-148) and the Health Care and Education Reconciliation Act of 2010 (Public Law 111-152).

Notes: Those provisions do not apply to the prescription drug spending of enrollees with low-income subsidies or enrollees who are in plans that receive the retiree drug subsidy. n.a. = not applicable.

Distribution of Spending in Medicare Part D

Enrollees pay premiums to Part D plans and also pay deductibles, coinsurance, and copayments to pharmacies under the program. (Those premiums and cost-sharing requirements may be covered by third parties, such as charities or employers.) Medicare pays a premium subsidy to drug plans for all enrollees and additional subsidies for premiums and cost-sharing for low-income enrollees. All together, those payments to plans and pharmacies totaled $59.8 billion in 2007.[7] (That amount excludes prescription drug spending under plans that receive the retiree drug subsidy.) Enrollees paid 9 percent of that total amount in premiums to plans and 19percent in out-of-pocket payments to pharmacies (see Figure 1), for a total of 28 percent.[8] The Part D program paid 28 percent of the total for low-income subsidies beyond the standard benefit, 25 percent for the standard benefit of enrollees receiving low-income subsidies, and 19 percent for the standard benefit of other enrollees.[9] In sum, the Part D program paid 72 percent of the total. (As a result of the recently enacted health care legislation, the share covered by Part D will increase gradually, reaching 75percent in 2019.)

The contribution from the Part D program differed greatly depending on whether an enrollee received a low-income subsidy. In 2007, 24 million people were enrolled in Part D (excluding those enrolled in plans that received the retiree drug subsidy). Low-income subsidies were provided to 38 percent (or 9 million) of the enrollees.[10] For those enrollees, the Part D program paid nearly all of the payments to plans and pharmacies. For enrollees who did not receive those subsidies, the Part D program paid about 40 percent of the payments to plans and pharmacies.

The Role of Private Plans in Medicare Part D

The Part D program was designed to have private plans compete for enrollees on the basis of price, access to prescription drugs, quality, and performance. Each year, plans submit bids to CMS for the cost of offering the standard benefit to an average enrollee. CMS calculates a base premium using the nationwide average bid and determines its subsidy payments on that basis. (Steps that reduce the average bid thus reduce Medicare's costs.) Enrollees must pay the base premium plus any difference between their plan's bid and the nationwide average bid. Thus, enrollees in costlier plans face higher-than-average premiums for standard Part D benefits, and enrollees in less expensive plans pay lower-than-average premiums.

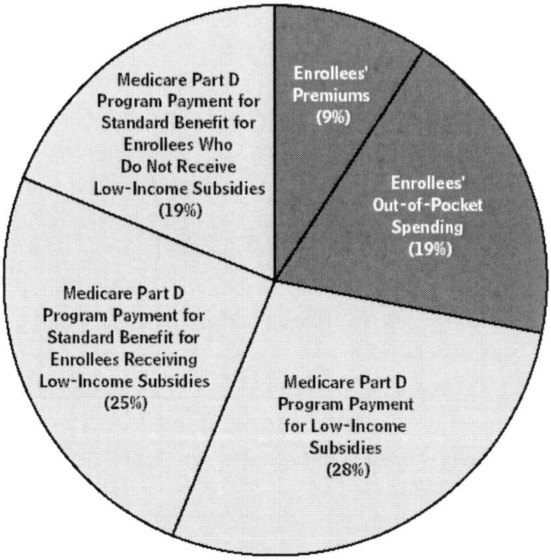

Source: Congressional Budget Office based on Medicare Board of Trustees, *2010 Annual Report of the Boards of Trustees of the Federal Hospital Insurance and Federal Supplementary Medical Insurance Trust Funds* (August 5, 2010), p. 186, Table IV.B10, and p. 189, Table IV.B11; information from the Office of the Actuary at the Centers for Medicare and Medicaid Services; and claims data (Prescription Drug Event data) reported to the Centers for Medicare and Medicaid Services by plans.

Notes: In dollars, the total payments to plans and pharmacies ($59.8 billion) breaks down into the following categories: $5.5 billion for enrollees' premiums, $11.4 billion for enrollees' out-of-pocket spending, $16.8 billion for the Medicare Part D program benefit for low-income subsidies, $14.6 billion for the Medicare Part D program payment for the standard benefit for enrollees receiving those subsidies, and $11.5 billion for the Medicare Part D program payment for the standard benefit for other enrollees.

Enrollees' out-of-pocket spending includes spending by other organizations (such as charitable organizations) on an enrollee's behalf.

Medicare Part D program payments for low-income subsidies include payments for premiums made by the Part D program to plans on behalf of enrollees receiving low-income subsidies.

Medicare Part D program payments exclude payments made under the retiree drug subsidy; those payments totaled about $4 billion in 2007.

Figure 1. Distribution of Payments to Plans and Pharmacies for Enrollees' Prescription Drug Spending Under Medicare Part D, 2007.

Plans try to reduce the cost of providing Part D benefits by managing enrollees' use of prescription drugs, by negotiating rebates with manufacturers of brand-name drugs, and by negotiating payment rates with pharmacies. Plans can perform those functions within their organization, but often they contract them out to pharmacy benefit managers (PBMs)—similar to the way that private health plans, including health maintenance organizations and employers' plans, often use PBMs to manage pharmacy benefits on their behalf.

Manage Enrollees' Use of Prescription Drugs. Many plans use tiered copayments to give enrollees incentives to follow a plan's formulary and to use less expensive drugs. A three-tier copayment structure is common: Enrollees pay a low copayment for generic drugs (the first tier), a higher one for preferred brand-name drugs (the second tier), and the highest copayment for nonpreferred brand-name drugs (the third tier). In 2007, the median copayments for stand-alone prescription drug plans were $5 for generic drugs, $28 for preferred brand-name drugs, and $60 for nonpreferred brand-name drugs.[11] (In the coverage gap, many enrollees must pay the full price for their drugs, so they may have even stronger financial incentives to use less costly drugs.)

Plans may also combine formularies with other rules—such as step therapy and prior authorization—to manage enrollees' use of prescription drugs. Step therapy requires that enrollees try a cheaper generic drug or preferred brand-name drug before using a more expensive non-preferred brand-name drug. The use of nonpreferred brand-name drugs may also require prior authorization from the plan, meaning that an enrollee's physician may have to explain why a more costly nonpreferred drug is required over a lower-cost generic or preferred brand.

About half of total prescription drug spending under Part D is on behalf of enrollees with low-income subsidies. Because those enrollees have very little cost sharing, a tiered copayment structure that relies on financial incentives may not be as effective in steering their drug use. Even so, rules such as step therapy and prior authorization could still be used to manage their drug use.

Negotiate Rebates with Manufacturers. Plans (or PBMs acting on their behalf) also use formularies to negotiate rebates with manufacturers of brand-name drugs. In developing its formulary, a plan determines which drugs are therapeutically similar. Then, for brand-name drugs with one or more close substitutes, the plan negotiates with manufacturers for rebates to be paid to the plan in return for placing manufacturers' drugs on the plan's preferred drug list.

In general, rebates are paid to plans for single-source brand-name drugs that are in classes containing similar drugs from which to choose. Rebates are typically not paid to plans (or are small) for multiple-source brand-name drugs and generic drugs. Once a drug is available in a generic version, pharmacists can dispense either the generic or the brand. At that point, prescription drug plans are not in a position to promote either the multiple-source brand-name drug or the generic version, so they do not typically receive rebates on them.

Restrictive formularies that list fewer drugs in each therapeutic class will generate higher rebates than less restrictive formularies that list several drugs in each therapeutic class, because plans with more restrictive formularies will be better able to steer enrollees to a particular manufacturer's drug and away from the drug's competitors. Plans with more restrictive formularies may be less attractive to enrollees, however.

Pharmaceutical manufacturers paid rebates to prescription drug plans under Part D that totaled about $6 billion in 2007. Costs of single-source brand-name drugs in that year totaled about $44 billion in the Part D program. If the $6 billion in rebates were paid primarily for single-source brand-name drugs, then rebates constituted about 14 percent of the cost of those drugs. (Unless otherwise indicated, figures for total prescription drug costs are net of those rebates.)

Negotiate Payment Rates with Pharmacies. Plans (or PBMs acting on their behalf) negotiate payment rates with pharmacies and seek discounts in exchange for including pharmacies in their networks. Drugs purchased at pharmacies outside a plan's network may not be covered or may require a higher copayment or coinsurance rate.

Pharmacies may be willing to accept lower payments per prescription in exchange for the greater volume of sales that can result from being part of a plan's pharmacy network. The plan's ability to achieve large discounts is greater the more restrictive the pharmacy network. However, like restrictive formularies, an overly restrictive pharmacy network may make a plan less attractive to enrollees.

Restrictions on Private Plans in Medicare Part D. Plans must meet certain requirements that limit their ability to reduce the costs of providing Part D benefits. Those requirements are intended to ensure that enrollees have access to the drugs that they need and to prevent plans from discouraging beneficiaries with high drug costs from enrolling. For example, some requirements concern how many drugs in a category or class of drugs must be covered; others involve having an adequate pharmacy network.

Classification systems for drugs are used by plans when developing their formularies. The classification systems group drugs into therapeutic categories and pharmacologic classes of drugs that work in a similar way or are used to treat the same condition.[12] There are many different classification systems. "Model Guidelines" is one such system specifically developed for Medicare Part D.[13] Plans may adopt the Model Guidelines or may use their own classification system. A plan's formulary must include at least two drugs in each therapeutic category and class and must include all, or substantially all, of the drugs in the following six "protected" categories or classes: anti-convulsant, antidepressant, antineoplastic, antipsychotic, antiretroviral, and immunosuppressant.

Generic Drugs in Medicare Part D

CBO examined the use of generic drugs in Medicare Part D for calendar year 2007 using a sample of claims data containing about 10 million prescription records submitted by plans to the Centers for Medicare and Medicaid Services.[14] (For a description of the claims data used in the analysis, see the appendix.) CBO analyzed how much was saved as a result of the use of generic drugs and the potential for savings from increasing the use of those drugs. The analysis examined savings from generic substitution—substituting a chemically equivalent generic drug for a brand-name drug. It also examined one form of therapeutic substitution—namely, substituting a generic drug for a brand-name drug when the generic is not chemically equivalent to the brand but is in the same therapeutic class. Therapeutic substitution can also include substituting a lower priced brand for a higher priced brand that is in the same therapeutic class, but that approach is beyond the scope of this report. (For information about the role of generic drugs in the U.S. pharmaceutical marketplace more generally, see Box 1.)

Generic Substitution

In 2007, about 65 percent of Part D prescriptions were filled with generic drugs, but those prescriptions accounted for about one-quarter of total prescription drug costs (see Table 2 on page 12).[15] By contrast, 30 percent of Part D prescriptions were filled with single-source brand-name drugs, but those prescriptions accounted for 68 percent of total prescription drug costs. Among Part D prescriptions written for multiple-source drugs (drugs that are available in brand-name and generic versions), more than 90 percent were filled with the generic option. That figure reflects the strong financial incentives for plans to encourage the use of generic drugs and for enrollees to use generics when available.

Table 2. Share of Part D Prescriptions and Prescription Drug Costs, by Drug Type, 2007

Drug Type	Percentage of Prescriptions	Percentage of Prescription Drug Costs
Generic	65	25
Multiple-Source Brand	5	7
Single-Source Brand	30	68
Total	100	100

Source: Congressional Budget Office based on Medicare Part D Prescription Drug Event claims data for 2007 provided by the Centers for Medicare and Medicaid Services and rebate data from the Medicare Board of Trustees, *2010 Annual Report of the Boards of Trustees of the Federal Hospital Insurance and Federal Supplementary Medical Insurance Trust Funds* (August 5, 2010), p. 185.

Note: Multiple-source brand refers to a drug that is sold under a brand name but is also available in generic versions from other manufacturers. Single-source brand refers to a drug that is sold under a brand name and is under patent protection—and thus is available from only one manufacturer (or occasionally from other manufacturers under license from the patent holder) and for which no chemically equivalent generic version is available.

BOX 1. GENERIC DRUGS IN THE U.S. PHARMACEUTICAL MARKETPLACE

Generic drugs are chemically equivalent versions of brand-name drugs that can be approved under an abbreviated regulatory process once the brand's patent or other periods of exclusivity in the market expire (or the patent is successfully challenged). Manufacturers of generic drugs are not required to duplicate all of the costly clinical trials conducted by the manufacturer of the brand-name drug; instead, to gain approval from the Food and Drug Administration (FDA), they must demonstrate only that the generic version contains the same active ingredient as the brand-name version (inactive ingredients may vary) and provides very similar concentrations of the drug in the blood.[1] The FDA maintains that if blood concentrations are the same, the therapeutic effect will be the same, so there is no need to carry out studies for clinical effectiveness.[2] Even so, some groups of physicians have expressed concern that generic drugs may not work as well as their brand-name counterparts. For example, the American Academy of Neurology opposes the substitution of generic anticonvulsant drugs for the treatment of epilepsy without the attending physician's approval.[3]

As a result of the abbreviated regulatory process, several manufacturers of generic drugs typically enter the market when the law allows them to do so. As the number of manufacturers grows, price competition among them increases, and the average price of the generic drug relative to that of the brand-name drug declines. On average, the retail price of a generic drug is 75 percent lower than the retail price of a brand-name drug.[4] Accordingly, generic substitution—substituting a generic drug, when one is available, for a brand-name drug—is a major strategy that health insurers use to reduce their spending on prescription drugs.

Private health insurers can promote generic substitution by using a formulary (a list of covered drugs) combined with tiered copayments, charging the lowest copayment for generic drugs and a higher one for multiple-source brand-name drugs (brand-name drugs that have a generic form available). Some health insurers have formularies that exclude multiple-source brand-name drugs from coverage. However, those sorts of formularies are not very common. One 2004 survey found that about 20 percent of employees in the private sector with prescription drug benefits had no coverage for multiple-source brand-name drugs.[5]

Health insurers have help from pharmacists in promoting generic substitution. Generally, when a drug is available in both generic and brand-name forms, states' laws allow pharmacists to fill the prescription with the generic even when the physician has written the prescription for the brand-name drug. Federal regulations implementing the drug benefit under Part D of Medicare also require pharmacists to notify patients if a generic substitute is available. In most states, however, the pharmacist must obtain the consent of the patient or at least must inform the patient when a generic drug is being substituted. The pharmacist cannot dispense the generic drug if the physician indicates in writing on the prescription "no substitution" or that the brand is "medically necessary."[6]

1. In addition, the generic drug must be identical to the brand-name (or innovator) drug in strength, dosage form, and route of administration. It also must be indicated for the same uses; be bioequivalent; meet the same batch requirements for identity, strength, purity, and quality; and be manufactured under the same standards of the FDA's good manufacturing practice regulations required for brand-name products. See the FDA's Web site, www.fda.gov/Drugs/ResourcesForYou/ Consumers/BuyingUsingMedicineSafely/UnderstandingGenericDrugs/ ucm144456.htm.
2. See "Facts and Myths about Generic Drugs," www.fda.gov/ Drugs/ Resources ForYou/Consumers/BuyingUsingMedicineSafely/UnderstandingGeneric Drugs/ucm 167991.htm.
3. See K. Liow and others, "Position statement on the coverage of anticonvulsant drugs for the treatment of epilepsy," Neurology, vol. 68, no. 16 (April 17, 2007), pp. 1249–1250.
4. That information is based on average prescription drug costsT in 2007 from the National Association of Chain Drug Stores (www.nacds.org/wmspage.cfm? parm1= 6536, accessed January 11, 2010).
5. The Kaiser Family Foundation and the Health Research andT Educational Trust survey employers each year to examine trends in employment-based health coverage. The 2004 survey is the most recent one to include a question about mandatory use of generic drugs when available. See Kaiser Family Foundation and Health Research and Educational Trust, Employer Health Benefits: 2004 Annual Survey (Menlo Park, Calif., and Chicago, 2004).
6. Jack Hoadley,J Cost Containment Strategies for Prescription Drugs: Assessing the Evidence in the Literature (report prepared for the Henry J. Kaiser Family Foundation, March 2005), p. 32.

Those estimates for Part D of the percentage of prescriptions filled with generic drugs (65 percent) and the percentage of prescriptions written for multiple-source drugs that were filled with the generic option (more than 90percent) are similar to estimates from other studies of the U.S. market as a whole and of Medicaid. One study found that 69 percent of prescriptions in the United States were filled with generic drugs at the end of 2008.[16] Another study found that 89 percent of prescriptions written for multiple-source drugs were filled with the generic option under the Medicaid program in 2004.[17] Other industry observers have reported that 90 percent or more of prescriptions written for multiple-source drugs were filled with the generic option under plans in the private sector by 2006.[18]

Savings from Generic Substitution in Medicare Part D

CBO estimates that, in 2007, about $33 billion was saved because a generic drug was dispensed instead of its brand-name counterpart. Thus, total payments to plans and pharmacies from the Part D program and its enrollees would have been about $93 billion—or 55 percent higher—if no generics had been available. The estimate is based on the number of prescriptions filled with a generic drug and the observed difference between prices for brand-name drugs and the generic alternatives. The analysis holds several factors constant and reflects CBO's assessment that generic entry is not likely to have a substantial effect on either the price of the brand-name drug or the total quantity (including brand-name and generic versions) of the drug sold (see Box 2 on page 10).

Box 2. How Competition from Generic Drugs Affects Prices and Quantities of Prescription Drugs

Competition from generic drugs has varied and sometimes ambiguous effects on the quantity of a drug sold (including brand-name and generic versions) and the price of the brand-name version.

Effects on Prices

Researchers have found that the average prices of generic drugs are much lower than the prices of brand-name drugs. As more manufacturers of generic drugs enter the market, the average price of the generic drugs relative to that of the brand-name drug declines, and the market share of the generic drugs increases.[1]

The effect of generic competition on the price of the brand-name drug is less clear-cut. Some studies conclude that the price of the brand-name drug increases because of competition from generics. One explanation for that effect is that some consumers are less price-sensitive than others, especially if they perceive the quality of the brand-name drug to be higher than that of its generic competitors. According to that logic, manufacturers of generic drugs compete among themselves for the price-sensitive consumers; the brand-name manufacturer retains the less price-sensitive consumers and chooses to charge them a higher price for the brand-name drug than the price before generic entry.[2]

Other studies conclude that competition from generics exerts a downward pressure on the price of the brand-name drug. In this story, although the price of a brand-name drug typically increases over time after generics enter the market, the competition from generic entry causes the price of the brand-name drug to increase by less than it would have in the absence of generic entry.[3]

Regardless of how generic entry affects the price of the brand-name drug, the overall effect of generic entry is to decrease the average price of the drug (for brand-name and generic versions) because the prices of the generic drugs are so far below the price of the brand-name drug and because generic competitors capture a large share of the market.

Effects on Quantities

Typically, the total quantity of a drug sold might be expected to increase as a result of competition from generic versions because consumers typically buy more of a good when its price decreases. However, the total quantity of a drug sold may remain unchanged or may decline somewhat after generic competitors enter the market, for many reasons.[4] In response to anticipated generic entry, for example, manufacturers of the brand-name drug sometimes are able to modify it (by creating an extended-release version, for instance) and switch consumers to the modified and newly patented version before generic entry begins. Such a switch would reduce demand for the original drug.

A decline in sales could also result if the brand-name manufacturer decreases advertising for the drug. That often occurs when generic competitors enter the market because the brand-name manufacturer is no longer able to capture all the benefits of that advertising.[5] Consumers may switch to a competing brand-name drug that is still advertised, or consumers with the condition may no longer use any drug therapy. A decline in quantity also could be caused by newer brands coming on the market and replacing the older drug therapy (in which case the decline is unrelated to generic entry).

Researchers have found that the overall effect of generic entry is to lower total spending on the drug (for brand-name and generic versions) because the average price is much lower.[6]

Effects on Estimates of Savings

Based on research about the effects of generic entry, the Congressional Budget Office (CBO) concluded that generic entry is not likely to have a substantial effect on either the price of the brand-name drug or the total quantity (including brand-name and generic versions) of the drug sold. CBO's estimates of savings under Part D of Medicare from generic substitution—substituting a chemically equivalent generic drug for a brand-name drug—reflect that assessment. If, instead, competition from generic drugs caused brand-name manufacturers to raise their prices, then CBO's estimates of savings might be too high. Conversely, if competition from generics caused brand-name manufacturers to lower their prices, then CBO's estimates of savings might be too low.

The estimates would also change if generic entry led to changes in the quantity of a drug sold in a specific market. If the availability of cheaper generic drugs caused the total quantity of drugs sold to increase, then the estimates of savings might be too high. If the total quantity of drugs sold declined because consumers switched to modified and newly patented versions of the brand-name drug, then spending on those new versions would offset the estimated savings from generic substitution.

In addition, changes in the marketing strategy of pharmaceutical firms producing brand-name drugs and consumers' response to those changes could affect CBO's estimates. If competition from equivalent generic drugs reduced the incentive of the manufacturer of the brand-name drug to advertise and consumers therefore switched to competing brand-name drugs, then the estimates of savings might be too high (if the competing brand drugs have a higher price than the brand with generic equivalents). Or, the estimates of savings might be too low, if the price of the competing brand drugs was lower than the price of the brand with generic equivalents. Finally, if consumers discontinued drug therapy in response to lower levels of advertising, then the estimates of savings might be too low.

More broadly, if entry by generic drugs had been prohibited—that is, if patents for drugs were essentially permanent—the market for drugs could have evolved in different ways that are very hard to predict. The types of drugs available, their prices, and their utilization rates could differ from the observed experience in ways that are not captured by studies of generic entry. Because of the uncertainties involved in predicting what would happen in that counterfactual case, CBO has not factored those possibilities into its estimate of the savings that have been achieved from generic substitution.

1. See F.M. Scherer, "Pricing, Profits, and Technological Progress in the Pharmaceutical Industry," Journal of Economic Perspectives, vol. 7, no. 3 (Summer 1993), pp. 97–115.
2. See, for example, Henry Grabowski and John Vernon, "Brand Loyalty, Entry, and Price Competition in Pharmaceuticals After the 1984 Drug Act," Journal of Law and Economics, vol. 35 (October 1992), pp. 331–350; and Richard Frank and David Salkever, "Generic Entry and the Pricing of Pharmaceuticals," Journal of Economics and Management Strategy, vol. 6, no. 1 (Spring 1997), pp. 75–90.
3. See, for example, Richard Caves, Michael Whinston, and Mark Hurwitz, "Patent Expiration, Entry, and Competition in the U.S. Pharmaceutical Industry," Brookings Papers on Economic Activity: Microeconomics (1991), pp. 1–66; Jayanta Bhattacharya and William Vogt, "A Simple Model of Pharmaceutical Price Dynamics," Journal of Law and Economics, vol. 46 (October 2003); and Sara Fisher Ellison and others, "Characteristics of Demand for Pharmaceutical Products: An Examination of Four Cephalosporins," RAND Journal of Economics, vol. 28, no. 3 (Autumn 1997), pp. 426–446.
4. See Caves, Whinston, and Hurwitz, "Patent Expiration, Entry, and Competition in the U.S. Pharmaceutical Industry."
5. Ibid.; and Bhattacharya and Vogt, "A Simple Model of Pharmaceutical Price Dynamics."
6. See Caves, Whinston, and Hurwitz, "Patent Expiration, S Entry, and Competition in the U.S. Pharmaceutical Industry."

Based on the data that CBO analyzed, about 600 million prescriptions were filled with a generic drug in 2007. For about 500 million of those, a multiple-source brand-name drug was available. (A brand-name drug is not always available because the manufacturer may choose to exit the market after generic entry.) For those 500 million prescriptions, the average price (weighted by the number of generic prescriptions) of the multiple-source brand-name drugs was \$89 per prescription, whereas the average price of their generic counterparts was \$23 per prescription. The savings per prescription equals \$66—the difference between those two average prices. The savings per prescription multiplied by the 500 million prescriptions yields the estimate of about \$33 billion in savings (see Table 3 on page 13).[19]

The \$33 billion in savings was shared by enrollees and the Part D program through a combination of lower copayments and lower premiums than would have been charged otherwise, but determining the precise share that accrued to each payer is difficult. A reasonable estimate is that the savings were shared in the same proportion as total payments by those groups to plans and pharmacies in 2007 (see Figure 1 on page 4). On that basis, enrollees saved about \$9 billion (or 28 percent), and the Part D program saved about $24 billion (or 72 percent).

The actual split of the savings between enrollees and the Part D program depends on several factors: how the savings from switching to generic drugs affects spending across the different phases of coverage, such as the coverage gap and the range of spending above the catastrophic threshold; the mix of prices and copayments for generic drugs and their brand-name counterparts; and whether the use of generic drugs is different for enrollees who receive low-income subsidies than for the rest of the Part D population. As a result, the shares of savings for enrollees and the Part D program could have been higher or lower. For example, the share of savings that accrued to enrollees could have been higher than 28 percent if the savings from switching to generic drugs reduced spending in the coverage gap disproportionately. Alternatively, the share of savings that accrued to enrollees could have been less than 28 percent if the savings from switching to generic drugs disproportionately reduced spending for catastrophic coverage, because that spending is borne mostly by the Part D program.

Another complication in the analysis stems from the fact that plans were also encouraging therapeutic substitution to varying degrees (if only by using tiered copayments). Consequently, some of the $33 billion in savings attributed to generic substitution was instead a result of therapeutic substitution. However, the amount of savings attributable to each form of substitution cannot be calculated from the available data. Because not enough is known about enrollees' medical histories or the brand-name drugs they might have been prescribed initially, it is difficult to determine when therapeutic substitutions might have occurred.

Potential Additional Savings from Generic Substitution in Medicare Part D. Generic substitution has produced substantial savings for Part D prescription drug spending, but the potential for additional savings from increased generic substitution is comparatively small. If all prescriptions for multiple-source brand-name drugs had instead been filled using generic drugs, about $900 million—or less than 2 percent of total payments to plans and pharmacies from the Part D program and its enrollees—would have been saved in 2007, CBO estimates.

Table 3. Estimate of Realized Savings from Generic Substitution, 2007 (Dollars)

Savings per Prescription	
Average Price of Multiple-Source Brand-Name Drugs Weighted by the Number of Generic Prescriptions	89
Minus: Average Price of Generic Prescriptions	23
Savings per Prescription	
Equals: Average Savings per Prescription	66
Total Savings	
Average Savings per Prescription	66
Multiplied by: Number of Generic Prescriptions Filled When a Multiple-Source Brand-Name Drug Was Available (Millions)	500
Equals: Total Savings (Millions of dollars)	33,000

Source: Congressional Budget Office based on Medicare Part D Prescription Drug Event claims data for 2007 provided by the Centers for Medicare and Medicaid Services.

Note: Multiple-source brand refers to a drug that is sold under a brand name but is also available in generic versions from other manufacturers.

Table 4. Potential Additional Savings from Generic Substitution, 2007 (Dollars)

Savings per Prescription	
Average Price of Multiple-Source Brand-Name Drugs	89
Minus: Average Price of Generic Drugs Weighted by the Number of Multiple-Source Brand Prescriptions	69
Equals: Average Savings per Prescription	20
Total Potential Savings	
Average Savings per Prescription	20
Multiplied by: Number of Multiple-Source Brand Prescriptions Filled When a Generic Drug Was Available (Millions)	45
Equals: Total Potential Additional Savings (Millions of dollars)	900

Source: Congressional Budget Office based on Medicare Part D Prescription Drug Event claims data for 2007 provided by the Centers for Medicare and Medicaid Services.

Note: Multiple-source brand refers to a drug that is sold under a brand name but is also available in generic versions from other manufacturers.

That estimate was derived as follows. About 45 million prescriptions (or 5 percent) were filled with multiple-source brand-name drugs in 2007. Those drugs were most often dispensed when the difference between the price of the brand-name and generic drugs was relatively small. Specifically, the average price of multiple-source brand-name drugs was $89 per prescription, whereas the average price of their generic counterparts (weighted by the number of multiple-source brand-name prescriptions) was $69 per prescription. The savings per prescription equals the difference of about $20 in the average prices. The savings per prescription multiplied by the 45 million prescriptions results in about $900 million in potential additional savings from generic substitution (see Table 4 on page 14). Again, the analysis holds several factors constant and reflects CBO's assessment that generic entry is not likely to have a substantial effect on either the price of the brand-name drug or the total quantity (including brand-name and generic versions) of the drug sold.

The potential additional savings would have been shared by enrollees and the Part D program, but the amounts that would have accrued to each party are not known. Again, using the average shares of payments by enrollees and the Part D program to allocate those savings, about $250 million (or 28 percent) would have accrued to enrollees, and about $650 million (or 72 percent) would have accrued to the Part D program. Because the additional savings would have come from drugs for which the generic alternative was more expensive than average, however, the savings to the Part D program could have been less than 72 percent if the switch to a generic drug reduced enrollees' spending by a proportionately larger amount. For example, on the basis of the difference between the median copayments in 2007 for a preferred brand-name drug ($28) and for a generic drug ($5) and with other factors held constant, the switch from a multiple-source brand-name drug to a generic drug would have saved the enrollee $23, but the plan would have paid an additional $3. If the multiple-source brand-name drug was nonpreferred, an enrollee's savings from switching to a generic version would have been even higher.

Two considerations, however, limit the applicability of those examples. First, they apply only to prescription drug spending between the deductible and the initial coverage limit on behalf of enrollees without low-income subsidies. Nearly all of the potential additional savings on behalf of enrollees with low-income subsidies would have accrued to the Part D program because that program pays nearly all of their costs. Second, if many enrollees had made such switches, then the average share of drug costs paid by enrollees would have been reduced; although enrollees might have initially captured most of the resulting savings, the calculated actuarial value of the plan could have been increased as a result. In that case, CMS probably would have required plans to rebalance their copayment structures to maintain the same actuarial value as provided by the standard benefit design, which would have shifted some savings from enrollees to Medicare. Therefore, using the current shares of spending on Part D to allocate the savings represents a reasonable approximation of the likely outcome, at least on average.

Therapeutic Substitution

Single-source brand-name drugs under Part D in 2007 cost about $38 billion. Some savings could have been achieved from that group of drugs by switching enrollees from a higher priced brand-name drug to a lower priced brand-name or generic drug that is not chemically equivalent but is in the same therapeutic class, a practice known as therapeutic substitution.

Using a tool called the "Medicare Prescription Drug Plan Finder," CBO analyzed one form of therapeutic substitution—switching an enrollee from a single-source brand-name drug to the generic form of a different drug that is in the same therapeutic class. The main purpose of the Medicare Prescription Drug Plan Finder is to help Medicare beneficiaries compare the total prices of plans on the basis of the drugs they take—counting not only the premium they would have to pay but also each plan's cost-sharing requirements for those specific drugs.

The tool also indicates when generic versions of drugs are available and provides information to beneficiaries on lower priced drugs that could be substituted for higher priced drugs in 15 classes and subclasses. The majority of those classes and subclasses are for drugs that treat cardiovascular diseases (for example, high cholesterol and high blood pressure). Also included in the list are classes and subclasses of drugs that treat gastrointestinal diseases and allergies. CBO calculated potential savings from therapeutic substitution for 7 of the 15 therapeutic classes identified by the drug finder as offering opportunities for such substitution (see Table 5 on page 15). Those seven classes were chosen because they contained at least one single-source brand-name drug and one therapeutically similar drug that was also available in a generic form. There were about 180million prescriptions written for drugs in the seven classes and subclasses in 2007, totaling about $10 billion in prescription drug costs. That amount represents about 17 percent of total payments to plans and pharmacies from the Part D program and its enrollees. About 66 percent of the prescriptions in the seven classes were dispensed with generic drugs, accounting for 36 percent of prescription drug costs in those classes. About 30percent of the prescriptions were filled with single-source brand-name drugs, which were 59 percent of prescription drug costs in those classes (see Table 6 on page 16).

For prescriptions written for multiple-source drugs, 95 percent were filled with the generic option. Focusing on those seven therapeutic classes, CBO determined that switching a prescription in 2007 from a single-source brand-name drug to a generic drug in the same class would have reduced the cost of each prescription by about 70 percent, on average. On the one hand, the potential to increase savings through therapeutic substitution would have been limited by the number of single-source prescriptions that it would have been medically appropriate to switch. On the other hand, savings might also have been feasible in other classes of drugs, but the difference in prices and the extent of the opportunities for therapeutic substitution would have differed in those classes.

Table 5. Selected Classes of Drugs Analyzed for Possible Therapeutic Substitution

Cardiovascular Agents
HMG CoA reductase inhibitors (statins)
Angiotensin-converting enzyme (ACE) inhibitors
Calcium channel blocking agents, dihydropyridines
Calcium channel blocking agents, nondihydropyridines
Nonselective beta-adrenergic blocking agents
Gastrointestinal Agents
Proton pump inhibitors
Respiratory Tract Agents
Mildly/nonsedating histamine1 (H1) blocking agents

Source: Congressional Budget Office based on information provided by the Centers for Medicare and Medicaid Services.

Notes: The Congressional Budget Office selected these seven classes and subclasses because they contained at least one single-source brand drug and a therapeutically similar drug that is also available in a generic form in 2007. Single-source brand refers to a drug that is sold under a brand name and is under patent protection—and thus is available from only one manufacturer (or occasionally from other manufacturers under license from the patent holder) and for which no chemically equivalent generic version is available.

This analysis excludes combination drugs and drugs that have alpha receptor activity or intrinsic sympathomimetic activity.

Table 6. Percentage of Part D Prescriptions and Prescription Drug Costs, by Drug Type, in Seven Selected Classes and Subclasses, 2007

Drug Type	Percentage of Prescriptions	Percentage of Prescription Drug Costs
Generic	66	36
Multiple-Source Brand	4	5
Single-Source Brand	30	59
Total	**100**	**100**

Source: Congressional Budget Office based on Medicare Part D Prescription Drug Event claims data for 2007 provided by the Centers for Medicare and Medicaid Services and rebate data from the Medicare Board of Trustees, *2010 Annual Report of the Boards of Trustees of the Federal Hospital Insurance and Federal Supplementary Medical Insurance Trust Funds* (August 5, 2010), p. 185.

Note: Multiple-source brand refers to a drug that is sold under a brand name but is also available in generic versions from other manufacturers. Single-source brand refers to a drug that is sold under a brand name and is under patent protection—and thus is available from only one manufacturer (or occasionally from other manufacturers under license from the patent holder) and for which no chemically equivalent generic version is available.

Potential Savings from Therapeutic Substitution in Certain Drug Classes

Prescription drug spending for single-source drugs totaled about $5.8 billion (net of rebates) in 2007 in the seven classes that CBO considered. In the claims data that CBO analyzed, the price of a single-source brand-name drug was $128 per prescription, on average. Because plans received rebates from manufacturers that averaged about 14 percent of single-source prescription drug spending, the average price of a single-source brand-name prescription minus rebates was about $110. The average price of generic drugs in those seven classes (weighted by the number of single-source prescriptions in each class) was $34 per prescription, or about 70percent lower than the average price of the single-source brand-name drugs. Thus, the average savings per prescription from switching equals $76.

There were 53 million single-source brand-name prescriptions in those classes. If all had been switched to generics from the same class, then multiplying by the savings per prescription would yield a potential reduction in prescription drug spending of about $4 billion (see Table 7 on page 17).[20] That reduction would have been about 7percent of total payments to plans and pharmacies from the Part D program and its enrollees in 2007. The analysis holds several factors constant and reflects CBO's assessment that generic entry is not likely to have a substantial effect either on the price of the brand-name drug or on the total quantity (including brand-name and generic versions) of the drug sold.

The potential reduction of $4 billion in prescription drug spending would have been shared by enrollees and the Part D program. Again applying the shares of payments by those groups to plans and pharmacies in 2007 (see Figure 1 on page 4), enrollees' spending would have been reduced by $1.1 billion (or 28 percent), and the Part D program's spending would have been reduced by $2.9 billion (or 72 percent). The shares of those savings that would have accrued to both parties could have been higher or lower in actuality, however. In particular, shares of savings for any subset of therapeutic classes could have differed from average shares calculated for all classes.

Table 7. Potential Savings from Therapeutic Substitution for Seven Selected Drug Classes, 2007 (Dollars)

Savings per Prescription	
Average Price of Single-Source Brand-Name Drugs, Net of Rebates[a]	110
Minus: Average Price of Generic Drugs Weighted by the Number of Single-Source Brand Prescriptions	34
Equals: Potential Additional Savings per Prescription	76
Total Potential Savings[b]	
Potential Additional Savings per Prescription	76
Multiplied by: Number of Single-Source Brand Prescriptions Filled When a Generic Drug Was Available (Millions)	53
Equals: Total Potential Savings[b] (Millions of dollars)	4,028

Source: Congressional Budget Office based on Medicare Part D Prescription Drug Event claims data for 2007 provided by the Centers for Medicare and Medicaid Services and rebate data from the Medicare Board of Trustees, *2010 Annual Report of the Boards of Trustees of the Federal Hospital Insurance and Federal Supplementary Medical Insurance Trust Funds* (August 5, 2010), p. 185.

Note: Single-source brand refers to a drug that is under patent protection and is sold under a brand name—and thus is available from only one manufacturer (or occasionally from other manufacturers under license from the patent holder). No chemically equivalent generic version is available.

a. Plans received rebates from manufacturers that averaged about 14 percent of single-source prescription drug costs in 2007.

b. Potential savings are higher than the actual amount would be; in many cases, it would be medically inappropriate to switch a patient's prescription from a single-source brand in one of the seven classes to a generic in the same class.

Medical Appropriateness of Therapeutic Substitution

The savings that feasibly could have been achieved from therapeutic substitution in those classes of drugs would have been smaller than $4 billion because it would have been medically inappropriate, in many cases, to make such switches. Within a therapeutic class, drugs may be approved by the Food and Drug Administration (FDA) to treat different symptoms and diseases. For example, within the class of drugs known as "nonselective beta-adrenergic blocking agents" (used for treating high blood pressure) is a subset of drugs that is also approved for treating migraines. The physician of a patient with migraines may not be willing to write a new prescription for a generic drug in that class of blocking agents if the drug has not been approved by the FDA to treat migraines.

Even among drugs approved to treat the same condition, important differences can exist. Some drugs in a class may be more effective than others, at least for some members of the population. Certain subpopulations—for example, people with liver or kidney disease—may need a specific brand-name drug in a class. In addition, some drugs in a class may have harmful side effects for different patients. Depending on the drug, side effects can range from relatively mild (such as dry mouth and drowsiness) to more severe (such as nausea and headaches) to life threatening (such as seizures, difficulty breathing, and liver damage). Moreover, drugs may have different dosing regimens, and physicians may be concerned about a reduction in patient compliance if they switched to drugs that must be taken more frequently. Also, physicians and their patients may be reluctant to switch to a therapeutic alternative once a condition has been stabilized using a brand-name drug. Finally, physicians' clinical experience with their patients may lead them to conclude that certain patients respond better to a particular drug from a given class.

Reflecting those considerations, a pharmacist must obtain the consent of the prescribing physician before substituting a generic drug for a single-source drug that is not chemically equivalent but is in the same therapeutic class. In contrast, a pharmacist can generally substitute a chemically equivalent generic drug for its brand-name counterpart without contacting the physician.

The claims data that CBO used do not contain enough information to determine the percentage of prescriptions for which therapeutic substitution would have been medically appropriate. That analysis would require detailed information about the incidence of diseases and other conditions in the Part D population and a thorough review of disease-treatment guidelines. However, examining potential savings by class provides some additional insight. Almost all of the potential savings from therapeutic substitution were concentrated in two of the seven classes that CBO examined: Proton pump inhibitors accounted for about 50 percent of the potential savings, and statins accounted for 44 percent. That concentration of savings resulted from the high percentages of prescriptions filled with single-source brand-name drugs in the two classes relative to the others—as well as the large number of prescriptions written for those widely used drugs.

Proton pump inhibitors are used to treat chronic symptoms of heartburn or acid regurgitation (known as gastro- esophageal reflux disease) and to treat and prevent ulcers.[21] Research indicates that drugs in that class are similar in safety and effectiveness when compared at equivalent doses.[22] That finding would indicate that a large share of single-source prescriptions could be switched to generic proton pump inhibitors.

Statins are used to lower cholesterol. High cholesterol can increase the risk of a heart attack and death from heart disease or stroke. Statins differ by how much of a reduction in cholesterol they provide. Enrollees who require large reductions to achieve desired blood concentrations would probably require a brand-name statin.[23] Although one health plan reported that more than 75 percent of patients taking a statin could achieve their cholesterol-lowering goals using a generic statin, specific information on the population of Medicare enrollees taking single-source brand-name statins would be needed to determine if the use of generic drugs could be increased among that population.[24]

Application to other Drug Classes. For other reasons, potential savings from therapeutic substitution could have been higher than $4 billion. The seven classes that CBO examined accounted for only 17 percent of total prescription drug costs in 2007 and only about 15percent of the costs of single-source brand-name drugs under Part D. To the extent that other classes also present opportunities for therapeutic substitution, potential savings would increase. Additionally, this analysis considered just one form of therapeutic substitution. If potential savings from substituting lower priced brands for higher priced brands in the same therapeutic class were also considered, then those savings would increase.

The range of rates for the utilization of generic drugs across plans in Part D may provide some insight into the potential for switching prescriptions from single-source brands to generic alternatives across all therapeutic classes. Although the overall share of prescriptions filled with generic drugs was about 65 percent under Part D in 2007, it generally ranged from about 55 percent to about 70 percent among stand-alone drugs plans, and it reached somewhat higher rates in some integrated health plans—indicating that the degree to which plans are promoting the use of generics over brands varies widely, so there may be room for plans with low rates of generic utilization to increase them.[25] (However, the differences in rates of generic utilization could also stem from differences in the population of enrollees in each plan.)

Comparing Potential Savings from Generic and Therapeutic Substitution

CBO's analysis of claims data from 2007 indicates that the potential for additional reductions in prescription drug spending is greater with therapeutic substitution than with the more straightforward generic substitution—although as noted above, the challenges in achieving those savings may also be greater for therapeutic substitution. In that analysis, therapeutic substitution resulted in higher savings primarily because the cost of a generic prescription was about 70 percent lower than that of a single-source brand-name prescription in the same therapeutic class (for the classes examined), whereas the cost of a generic prescription was only about 20 percent lower than the cost of a multiple-source brand-name prescription, on average.

Several factors explain that difference in potential savings. First, single-source brand-name drugs are generally newer and often represent improvements (real or perceived) over multiple-source brand-name drugs that treat the same condition, and their patent protection thus allows their manufacturers to charge prices that are typically higher than those charged for older drugs; that increases the potential savings from therapeutic substitution. Furthermore, when multiple-source brand-name drugs were dispensed, the prices of their generic counterparts were higher than the average price of all generic drugs that had been dispensed, which limits the potential additional savings from generic substitution. Moreover, the number of prescriptions under Part D that could be switched to a generic drug through therapeutic substitution was slightly greater than the number that could be switched through generic substitution—largely reflecting the extensive use of generic substitution that has already occurred. An offsetting consideration is that it would be medically inappropriate to practice therapeutic substitution in many cases, which is one factor that would reduce the actual savings that could be obtained from that approach.

Policymakers would face several challenges in developing tools to achieve any additional savings from the expanded use of generic drugs—particularly in the case of therapeutic substitution. About half of Part D spending is on behalf of enrollees who have lower income and thus qualify for additional subsidies.

Policies that used financial incentives to steer enrollees toward certain drugs might not be effective on that population because Medicare pays nearly all of their costs. In addition, plans must meet certain requirements intended to ensure that enrollees have access to the drugs that they need and to prevent the plans from discouraging beneficiaries with high drug costs from enrolling; those requirements limit plans' ability to steer drug use. Finally, it could be difficult for policymakers to design policies so that switches from single-source brand-name drugs to generic drugs were made only when medically appropriate.

Implications of Future Developments

The estimates of actual savings from generic substitution and potential savings from additional generic and therapeutic substitution in 2007 provide some insight into how much savings could be obtained in the future through the increased use of generic drugs. However, some changes in the pharmaceutical marketplace have already occurred—and many others could occur—that might affect actual and potential savings from the increased use of generic drugs. In addition, changes introduced by the recently enacted health care legislation will direct a larger share of any savings that are achieved to the Medicare Part D program because the program will cover an increasing share of prescription drug spending as the coverage gap closes.

Two factors may hold down prescription drug spending in the near term. First, payers will benefit from a wave of brand-name drugs in high-priced therapeutic classes losing patent protection or other periods of exclusivity, allowing first-time generic entry. Second, relatively few new brand-name drug products are expected to reach the market over the next few years.

A countervailing factor is that analysts expect to see a rapid increase in spending under Part D for a particular category of drugs called biologics. Those drugs, which are derived from living organisms, can be particularly expensive. The recently enacted health care legislation created a regulatory pathway for approving less expensive alternatives to those drugs, but in certain circumstances enrollees in Part D may have limited incentives to use them and drug plans may have limited incentives to encourage their use.

First-Time Generic Entry

Over the past several years, more brand-name drugs have become available in generic form, and the dollar value of sales of brand-name drugs that face generic competition has increased accordingly. Brand-name drugs with U.S. retail sales totaling roughly $21 billion in 2007, representing 11 percent of the U.S. retail market in that year, experienced first-time generic entry in 2008 and 2009 (see Figure 2). Drugs accounting for another $43 billion in U.S. retail sales, representing a further 21 percent of the U.S. retail market in 2007, will be subject to first-time generic entry during 2010 through 2012. Within Part D, the cost of those drugs was about $20 billion—equal to 33 percent of total payments to plans and pharmacies from the Part D program and its enrollees in 2007.

The introduction of more generic drugs increases the amount of savings that could be derived under Part D from their use. If the patterns of generic use and price differentials observed in 2007 were to continue, then 93percent of those brand-name prescriptions would be switched to the generic version at a price 74 percent less than that of the brand-name versions. Applying those percentages to the 2007 data on drug spending yields an estimate of about $14 billion in additional savings under Part D. That amount represents a 42 percent increase in the $33 billion in savings estimated from generic substitution in 2007.

Because those calculations use 2007 data, they represent an estimate of the additional savings that could have accrued in 2007 if single-source drugs that will lose patent protection by 2012 had been available in generic form in 2007. Both of those savings estimates—the $14 billion and the $33 billion—would be higher if calculated for future years because of inflation in drug prices and the likely growth in the number of Part D enrollees and prescriptions filled. Because the price of generic drugs relative to the price of brand-name drugs declines as more manufacturers of generic drugs enter the market, the additional savings from new generic entry would also be achieved over time rather than realized immediately.

Those trends in generic drug entry also affect the estimates of how much in additional savings could be achieved either through more generic substitution or from therapeutic substitution. The calculations above assumed that 7 percent of prescriptions would have been filled with multiple-source brand-name drugs, even though generics were newly available at a price 22 percent less than the price of the brand-name drug. If all of those prescriptions were instead filled with generic drugs, about $300 million in additional savings would be generated from generic substitution. That amount (which was also calculated using 2007 claims data and relative drug prices) represents a 33 percent increase in the $900 million in potential savings from additional generic substitution in 2007.

A further complication is that some of the brand-name drugs experiencing first-time generic entry are in one of the seven classes for which CBO calculated savings from therapeutic substitution. The single-source drugs that will face new generic entry accounted for about $2.5 billion of the $4 billion in potential savings from such substitution estimated for 2007. After that generic entry occurs, savings from those drugs would be included in CBO's estimate of savings and potential additional savings from generic substitution, so potential savings from therapeutic substitution would be reduced by their contribution. In other words, the $2.5 billion in lost savings from therapeutic substitution arises from part of the $14 billion in additional savings that CBO estimated to stem from new generic substitution.

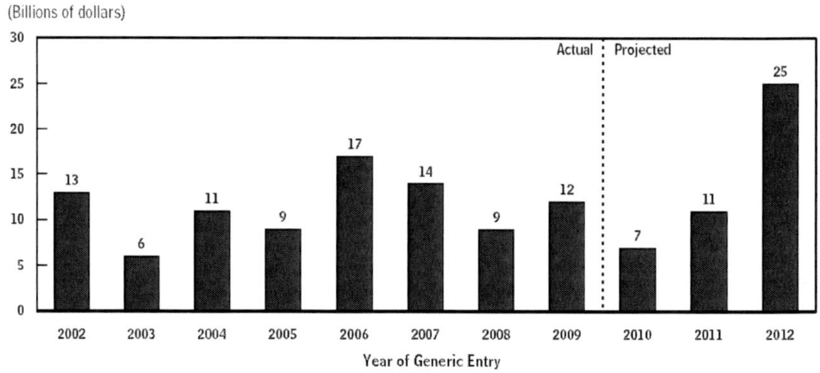

Source: Congressional Budget Office based on Medco's *Drug Trend Reports* from 2002 through 2010.

Note: For the years from 2002 through 2008, retail sales are reported for the year before generic entry. For the years from 2009 through 2012, retail sales are reported for 2007.

Figure 2. U.S. Retail Sales of Brand-Name Drugs Before First-Time Generic Entry.

Then again, some of the generic entry that is expected through 2012 will create new opportunities for substitution in three additional therapeutic classes.[26] Although the Medicare Prescription Drug Plan Finder identifies opportunities for possible therapeutic substitutions in those three classes, they were not included in CBO's calculation of potential savings from therapeutic substitution in 2007 because they currently contain only single-source drugs. In other words, the generic drugs in those classes would be first-in-class generics and create opportunities for the type of therapeutic substitution that CBO examined.

However, the potential savings from therapeutic substitution in those three classes would be small. The potential savings associated with entry of those generic drugs was estimated as follows. Single-source brand-name drugs totaling about $0.3 billion in prescription drug spending in 2007 would be candidates for therapeutic substitution. If enrollees' prescriptions for all of those single-source brand-name drugs were switched to the new generic drugs in their classes at a price about 70 percent less than the price of the brand-name drugs, then an additional $0.2 billion would be saved through therapeutic substitution. On net, potential savings from therapeutic substitution in 10 therapeutic classes would decline from the $4 billion calculated for 2007 to $1.7 billion, or by 60 percent. Moreover, in many cases, it would be medically inappropriate to practice therapeutic substitution, which is one factor that would reduce the actual savings that could be obtained.

New Brand-Name Drugs

The rate of introduction of new brand-name drugs is another major factor that will affect potential savings from generic drugs in the future. The introduction of new brand-name drugs can increase the utilization of single-source brand-name drugs and decrease savings from generic drugs, although the precise effect will depend on how big a share of the Part D market the new drugs can capture—and whether they shift drug utilization from existing therapies or largely establish new categories of spending. New drugs that are first in class (or breakthrough drugs) and treat a high-prevalence condition among Part D enrollees could gain a significant share of the Part D market. If enrollees switch from generic drugs to those new drugs, the opportunities for generic substitution would decline—at least until the new single-source drug loses patent protection. Moreover, if the new drug is truly superior, then opportunities for therapeutic substitution would not arise. Conversely, new drugs that enter into a crowded therapeutic class and that have little benefit over existing therapies for most people or that treat a low-prevalence condition among Part D enrollees may not gain much of a share of the Part D market and thus may have only a limited impact on projected savings from using generic drugs.

In the near term, first-time generic entry is expected to have a bigger impact on potential savings than the introduction of new brand-name drugs because the sales of new brand-name drugs are expected to be smaller than the sales of existing brands experiencing first-time generic entry.

Biologics

Spending under Part D on the category of drugs called biologics is expected to increase rapidly in the future. Those drugs can be particularly expensive, with prices reaching tens of thousands of dollars per patient each year. Because most biologics are injected or infused directly into the patient, they are more likely to be covered under Part B of Medicare. Consequently, biologics accounted for only about 6 percent of total prescription drug costs under Part D in 2007.[27] Between 2006 and 2007, however, spending on biologics under Part D grew by about 36 percent, whereas total Part D spending grew by 22 percent, according to the Medicare Payment Advisory Commission.[28] A higher rate of growth for Part D spending on biologics is expected to persist because of the continuing rapid increase in the price of biologics (compared with the prices of traditional drugs), greater use of existing biologics, and the large number of biologics under development.[29]

Provisions of the recently enacted health care legislation will partially mitigate that spending increase by creating a regulatory pathway for licensing products that are "biosimilar" to brand-name biologics. Unlike generic drugs, which contain the same active chemical ingredient as the original patented drug contains, biosimilars are similar to—but not exact copies of—much more complex molecules.

Potential savings in Part D from biosimilar drugs may be limited, however, for several reasons. In certain circumstances, enrollees and plans in Part D may have reduced incentives to use biosimilars. The process of designing and manufacturing biosimilars is complex and more costly than it is for traditional generic drugs, so the price discounts for biosimilars will not be as high in percentage terms as those for traditional generic drugs.[30] Specifically, CBO estimated that prices for biosimilars would ultimately be about 40 percent lower than prices of the original drugs—although the higher average prices for biologic products mean that the dollar differences in prices could still be quite large. The ability of plans to steer utilization toward biosimilars will also play an important role in determining the extent to which savings are realized under Part D. One potential constraint to that ability is that enrollees with low-income subsidies make up a disproportionately large share of the market for biologics under Part D. Because that group has nominal cost sharing, plans would probably need to use tools other than cost sharing (such as step therapy and prior authorization) to steer use toward biosimilars.

Another important issue is whether biosimilars will be treated in the same manner as generic drugs under Part D as the coverage gap is filled in. In particular, CMS has not yet issued guidance on how biosimilars will be classified for purposes of coverage determination in the range of spending that (under prior law) represented the coverage gap. If biosimilars are classified in the same category as generic drugs, enrollees without low-income subsidies and their plans may have incentives to purchase brand-name biologics over biosimilars. Because plans would pay a higher share of the cost of biosimilars than of brand-name biologics in that range of spending on behalf of enrollees without low-income subsidies (see Table 1), plans would probably pay more for biosimilars than for brand-name biologics. The discount provided by manufacturers of brand-name biologics will not only reduce costs to plans and enrollees but will also be counted toward the amount of spending required to reach the catastrophic threshold (at which point coverage is borne mostly by the Part D program), whereas no discount would be required of the manufacturer of the biosimilar. Only about 2 percent of enrollees without low-income subsidies reached that threshold in 2007, however, so that incentive will probably have a limited impact on total prescription drug spending under Part D.[31]

APPENDIX: DESCRIPTION OF DATA USED IN THIS ANALYSIS

This Congressional Budget Office (CBO) analysis of prescription drug spending is based on Medicare Part D Prescription Drug Event claims data for calendar year 2007.[32] Plans submit the claims data to the Centers for Medicare and Medicaid Services (CMS), which uses it to calculate a portion of Medicare's payments to plans. Each record in the data indicates a filled prescription and includes information about the enrollee, plan, pharmacy, and drug product dispensed. For this analysis, the main elements of interest are the product dispensed (identified by its national drug code number), days supplied, prices of the ingredients, dispensing fee paid to the pharmacy, and sales tax.

The claims data for 2007 include about 1 billion records, or prescriptions filled. The total cost for those prescriptions was $62.2 billion (including the prices for the ingredients, the dispensing fee, and the sales tax). For this analysis, CBO used a 1 percent sample of the claims data. The sample was constructed by first selecting a random sample of 1 percent of Part D enrollees and then selecting all the records on filled prescriptions for 2007 for those enrollees. CBO matched brand-name drugs with their chemically equivalent generic drugs in the sample using Thomson Micromedex's Red Book database. That database contains a code to identify drugs with common active ingredients, master dosage form, strength, and route of administration. It also contains information on list prices and other descriptive details on prescription and over-the-counter drugs. Using the additional information from the Red Book database, CBO was able to categorize the drugs as generic, multiple-source brand (brands with generic versions available), or single-source brand (brands without generic versions available).

The data do not include information on rebates from drug manufacturers. But according to the 2010 report of the Board of Trustees for the Medicare program, rebates for 2007 were approximately 9.6 percent of total prescription drug costs.[33] Applying that factor to total recorded cost produces an estimate of $56.2 billion for the total prescription drug cost net of rebates in 2007.

Total payments to plans and pharmacies by the Part D program and its enrollees ($59.8 billion) exceeded the total prescription drug cost net of rebates ($56.2 billion) by $3.6 billion in 2007. That difference in part reflects administrative expenses and profits of plans (including the costs of managing the drug benefit, which plans may do themselves or contract out to pharmacy benefit managers). However, that difference also reflects losses that plans incur on supplemental benefits that are offset by payments under other Medicare accounts.[34] The Medicare Board of Trustees estimates that actual administrative expenses and profits were about $4.3 billion in 2007 or roughly 13.5 percent of plans' benefit payments, which totaled about $32.4 billion.[35] Profits and administrative expenses as a percentage of plans' benefit payments are expected to decline slowly through 2019 because increases in prescription drug spending under Part D are estimated to be larger than increases in employee wages and the other input costs that affect plans' administrative expenses.[36]

End Notes

[1] The term "chemically equivalent generic" is used throughout this study to refer to a generic drug that the Food and Drug Administration has determined is identical or bioequivalent to a brand-name drug in dosage form, safety, strength, route of administration, quality, performance characteristics, and intended use.

[2] Figures exclude enrollees in and payments to plans that receive the retiree drug subsidy (a subsidy that Medicare provides to certain prescription drug plans offered by employers and union groups to their retirees). For details, see enrollment data for 2010, available at www.cms.gov/PrescriptionDrugCovGenIn/. Net outlays are spending on payment benefits minus payments from the states and the portion of premiums paid by enrollees through withholdings from Social Security benefits. (When Part D coverage began, the responsibility for paying for drugs for individuals who are enrolled in both Medicaid and

Medicare shifted from the Medicaid program to the Medicare Part D program. In recognition of that change, states are required to contribute to Part D a portion of their estimated avoided drug costs for that population.)

[3] Patient Protection and Affordable Care Act (Public Law 111-148) and Health Care and Education Reconciliation Act of 2010 (P.L. 111-152).

[4] In addition to Part D, Medicare consists of Parts A, B, and C, which pay for other health care services for seniors and people with disabilities. Part A covers inpatient hospital stays, skilled nursing facilities, home health care, and hospice care. Part B covers outpatient hospital care, doctors' services, and many other medical services not covered by Part A. The health care services offered under Parts A, B, and D (except hospice care) can be obtained through private health plans operating under Part C. For more information on Medicare, see Hinda Chaikind and others, *Medicare Primer,* CRS Report for Congress R40425 (Congressional Research Service, March 10, 2009).

[5] Medicare Payment Advisory Commission, *Report to the Congress: Medicare Payment Policy* (March 2008), p. 290 and p. 292; and *Report to the Congress: Medicare Payment Policy* (March 2010), p. 287.

[6] Enrollees qualifying for low-income subsidies are liable for additional costs if they choose plans with higher premiums than the limits set by the Centers for Medicare and Medicaid Services. Those limits ensure that enrollees will have at least one standalone drug plan available to them for which they do not have to pay a premium. See Patricia A. Davis, *Medicare Part D Prescription Drug Benefit,* CRS Report for Congress R40611 (Congressional Research Service, June 1, 2009), p. 12.

[7] Total payments to plans and pharmacies of $59.8 billion exceeded prescription drug costs net of rebates in 2007, which CBO estimated at $56.2 billion. The difference between the two amounts, in part, reflects administrative expenses and profits of plans. See the appendix for more details.

[8] Enrollees' premiums are the sum of premiums for the standard benefit and for enhanced benefits that have greater actuarial value. Premiums for the standard benefit (or a benefit of equal actuarial value to the standard benefit) are from Medicare Board of Trustees, *2010 Annual Report of the Boards of Trustees of the Federal Hospital Insurance and Federal Supplementary Medical Insurance Trust Funds* (August 5, 2010), p.189, Table IV.B11, the column labeled "Premiums." For enrollees with enhanced benefits, that report includes only a portion of their premiums—the amount they would have paid if they had received a benefit of equal value to the standard benefit. Information on additional premium amounts for enrollees with enhanced benefits, which amounted to $1.5billion in 2007, was provided by the Office of the Actuary at CMS.

Enrollees' out-of-pocket spending is based on data on prescription drug expenditures and includes spending in the categories "Patient Pay Amount" (amounts paid by enrollees), "Other True Out-of-Pocket (TrOOP)" (for example, amounts paid by a qualified State Pharmacy Assistance Program), and "Patient Liability Reduction Due to Other Payer Amount" (for example, amounts paid by programs for workers' compensation). "True Out-of-Pocket" refers to the requirement that enrollees must generally incur out-of-pocket costs themselves (and not be reimbursed by a third party) for those costs to count toward reaching the catastrophic threshold.

[9] Medicare Part D program payments to plans for the standard benefit are based on information provided by the Office of the Actuary at CMS. Part D program payments to plans for low-income subsidies are from Medicare Board of Trustees, *2010 Annual Report of the Boards of Trustees of the Federal Hospital Insurance and Federal Supplementary Medical Insurance Trust Funds* (August 5, 2010), p.186, Table IV.B10. They include payments for premiums, deductibles, coinsurance, and copayments made by the Part D program to plans on behalf of enrollees receiving low-income subsidies. Part D program payments exclude those made under the retiree drug subsidy, which, according to the same report, totaled about $4 billion in 2007.

[10] See Medicare Board of Trustees, *2010 Annual Report of the Boards of Trustees of the Federal Hospital Insurance and Federal Supplementary Medical Insurance Trust Funds,* p. 183.

[11] Patricia Neumana and Juliet Cubanski, "Medicare Part D Update—Lessons Learned and Unfinished Business," *New England Journal of Medicine,* vol. 361, no. 4 (July 23, 2009), p. 408.

[12] For example, Lipitor, a top-selling drug that lowers cholesterol, is in the "cardiovascular agents" therapeutic category. That category is further subdivided into pharmacologic classes. Lipitor is in the pharmacologic class "dyslipidemics."

[13] For more about the development of the Model Guidelines, see The USP Model Guidelines Expert Committee and U.S. Pharma-copeia Staff, "Narrative Review: The U.S. Pharmacopeia and Model Guidelines for Medicare Part D Formularies," *Annals of Internal Medicine,* vol. 145 (2006), pp. 448–453.

[14] Claims data from calendar year 2007 were the most recent available for Medicare Part D when CBO's analysis began.

[15] Estimates of generic utilization can vary depending on which database of drug information is used. CBO used Thomson Micromedex's Red Book database to classify prescription drugs as either brand-name or generic. Medi-Span and First DataBank also publish databases of drug information.

[16] Generic Pharmaceutical Association, *Generic Pharmaceuticals, 1999–2008: $734 Billion in Health Care Savings* (May 2009), p. 4.

[17] Department of Health and Human Services, Office of Inspector General, *Generic Drug Utilization in State Medicaid Programs,* OEI-05-05-00360 (July 2006), p. 7.

[18] Statement of Mark Merrit, Pharmaceutical Care Management Association, before the United States Senate Special Committee on Aging, *The Generic Drug Maze: Speeding Access to Affordable, Life Saving Drugs* (July 20, 2006).

[19] The estimate of savings from generic substitution does not include savings from the approximately 100 million prescriptions filled with a generic drug for which there is no alternative brand available because the brand's manufacturer exited the market. Those prescriptions represent about 4 percent of total prescription drug spending.

[20] The potential additional savings from therapeutic substitution are based on the difference between the price per prescription for the single-source brand-name drug and the average price per prescription for all generic drugs in the same therapeutic class. CBO also estimated savings for each class and subclass using other measures: the average price for a 30-day supply of generic drugs, the lowest price for a generic prescription, the lowest price for a 30-day supply of generic drugs, the price of the most frequently used generic prescription, and the price of the most frequently used generic drug based on the number of days supplied. The estimates of savings varied little between methodologies.

[21] Proton pump inhibitors are also available in low doses over the counter. Those versions are approved by the FDA only to treat infrequent symptoms of heartburn.

[22] Kenneth DeVault and Donald Castell, "Updated Guidelines for the Diagnosis and Treatment of Gastresophageal Reflux Disease," *American Journal of Gastroenterology,* vol. 100 (2005), pp. 190–200.

[23] Drug Effectiveness Review Project, Drug Class Review, *HMG-CoA Reductase Inhibitors (Statins) and Fixed-Dose Combination Products Containing a Statin, Final Report Update 5,* Oregon Health and Science University (November 2009).

[24] Emily Cox, Andy Behm, and Doug Mager, *2005 Generic Drug Trend Usage Report* (St. Louis, Mo.: Express Scripts).

[25] Rates of utilization of generic drugs by plan are based on data from CMS (see www.cms.hhs.gov/PrescriptionDrugCovGenIn/ 06_PerformanceData.asp#TopOfPage).

[26] Those additional classes are angiotensin II receptor antagonists and angiotensin II receptor antagonists/diuretic combinations (drugs in those classes treat cardiovascular diseases) and mildly/ nonsedating histamine1 (H1) blocking agents/decongestants (drugs in that class treat allergies).

[27] Medicare Payment Advisory Commission, *Report to the Congress: Improving Incentives in the Medicare Program* (June 2009), pp. 120–124.

[28] Ibid., p. 120.

[29] Congressional Research Service, *Follow-On Biologics: Intellectual Property and Innovation Issues,* CRS Report for Congress RL33901 (January 6, 2010).

[30] Congressional Budget Office, *Budget Options, Volume I: Health Care* (December 2008), pp. 126–128; and cost estimate for S. 1695, Biologics Price Competition and Innovation Act of 2007 (June 25, 2008).

[31] For the percentage of enrollees with spending that reached the coverage gap, see Medicare Payment Advisory Commission, *Report to the Congress: Medicare Payment Policy* (March 2010), p. 289.

[32] The claims data do not include prescription drug spending under plans that receive drug subsidies for retirees. In 2007, those subsidies totaled about $4 billion.

[33] Medicare Board of Trustees, *2010 Annual Report of the Boards of Trustees of the Federal Hospital Insurance and Federal Supplementary Medical Insurance Trust Funds* (August 5, 2010), p. 185.

[34] Some private plans provide Medicare Part D benefits that are integrated with other health care benefits (such as inpatient hospital stays and doctors' visits) traditionally provided under Parts A and B of Medicare. Those plans, called Medicare Advantage plans, are permitted to reduce premiums for prescription drug benefits and offer supplemental benefits using savings on Medicare payments for providing services under Parts A and B.

[35] Plans' benefit payments are for the standard benefit only. They include the Medicare Part D Program Payment for the standard benefit ($26.1 billion), enrollees' premiums for the standard benefit ($4.0 billion), and low-income subsidies for premiums ($2.3 billion). They do not include payments for supplemental benefits and low-income subsidies for cost sharing (deductibles, coinsurance, and copayments).

[36] See Medicare Board of Trustees, *2010 Annual Report,* p. 185, for projections of plans' administrative expenses and profits.

In: Medicare's Prescription Drug Program ISBN: 978-1-63463-122-8
Editor: Gloria R. Pattinson

Chapter 3

SPENDING PATTERNS FOR PRESCRIPTION DRUGS UNDER MEDICARE PART D*

Tamara Hayford

The centerpiece of the Medicare Prescription Drug, Improvement, and Modernization Act of 2003 (Medicare Modernization Act) was the creation of Medicare Part D, a subsidized pharmaceutical benefit that went into effect in 2006.[1] That additional coverage—which provides outpatient prescription drug insurance to seniors and to people under age 65 with certain disabilities—constituted the most substantial expansion of the Medicare program since its inception in 1965. In 2010, the federal government spent $62.0 billion on Part D, representing 12 percent of total federal spending for Medicare that year.[2]

Under Medicare Part D, all enrollees receive a subsidy for prescription drug insurance; an additional low-income subsidy (LIS) is available to enrollees with sufficiently low income and assets.[3] (In this issue brief, Part D enrollees who receive the LIS benefit are referred to as LIS enrollees; all others are referred to as non-LIS enrollees.) Enrollees in Part D choose a prescription drug insurance plan from a number of competing private plan sponsors. Total spending on Part D drugs equals the sum of spending by all payers combined, including plan sponsors, beneficiaries, the federal government, and third-party payers; in this brief, it is measured on a per-beneficiary basis.[4] In 2008—the most recent year for which data were

* This is an edited, reformatted and augmented version of an Economic and Budget Issue Brief issued by the Congressional Budget Office, December 2011.

available when the Congressional Budget Office (CBO) undertook this analysis—average spending for non-LIS enrollees was $1,800.[5] The amount of spending varied widely across enrollees in that category: for 7 percent, no spending occurred, whereas for 6 percent, the amount was at least $5,000. Enrollees who spent more tended to fill more prescriptions and more-expensive prescriptions. The federal government covered roughly 40 percent of nonLIS spending through premium subsidies, and beneficiaries covered most of the remainder through premium payments and out-of-pocket spending.

Average spending for LIS enrollees in 2008 was $3,600, double the spending for non-LIS enrollees. A slightly larger share of LIS enrollees (9 percent) had no Part D spending, but a much greater share (23 percent) had spending of at least $5,000. As with the non-LIS population, higher spending among LIS enrollees was driven by beneficiaries who filled more prescriptions and who filled more-expensive prescriptions. The higher spending among LIS beneficiaries most likely reflected that group's generally poorer health status and the more generous coverage available through the low-income subsidy. Because of that additional subsidy, the federal government covered 95 percent of LIS spending in 2008.

This issue brief reviews patterns of Medicare Part D utilization and spending among the non-LIS and LIS populations. Other important topics relating to Part D, such as the provision of public benefits by sponsors of private plans and competition among those sponsors, are beyond the scope of this analysis.

THE MEDICARE PART D PROGRAM

Before the creation of Part D, Medicare provided very limited coverage for the costs of outpatient prescription drugs.[6] As a result, the three-quarters of Medicare beneficiaries who had such coverage in the late 1990s obtained it from other sources; the remainder paid directly for all of their prescription drugs.[7] The patchwork of drug insurance options available at that time included public programs (such as Medicaid) and private insurance plans (such as employment-based plans for retirees and medigap plans that supplement Medicare). Whereas the poorest Medicare beneficiaries were often eligible for coverage under Medicaid, those with higher income were more likely to have employment-based plans or to purchase medigap policies. The "near poor"—those with incomes ranging from 100 percent to 200 percent of the federal poverty level—were disproportionately uninsured.

Anyone enrolled in traditional fee-for-service (FFS) Medicare (Parts A and B) or in Medicare Advantage (Part C) is eligible for prescription drug coverage under Part D. (Part A covers hospital insurance, and Part B covers physician visits and other outpatient services; those benefits are administered by the Centers for Medicare and Medicaid Services, or CMS. Part C combines the benefits provided under Parts A and B and is administered by private companies that contract with CMS.) The Medicare Part D benefit is similar to some parts of Medicare but different from others. As with Medicare Part B, people who enroll in Part D receive substantial federal subsidies, and people who do not enroll in Part D upon eligibility face higher premiums if they sign up late. Those features of the program provide a strong incentive for people to enroll upon becoming eligible.[8] Part D differs from FFS Medicare in that beneficiaries choose a drug plan from among a number of competing private plans. In that respect, Part D is similar to Medicare Advantage (known as Medicare+Choice before the Medicare Modernization Act was passed in 2003), under which enrollees choose among available private health plans for their Medicare benefits.

In the first six months after the program was implemented, 22.5 million Medicare beneficiaries, or 53 percent of the Medicare population, signed up for the Part D benefit.[9] Many of those enrollees may have previously had prescription drug coverage through another source: By CBO's estimates, in 1999, 16 percent of Medicare enrollees had prescription drug insurance through Medicaid and 14 percent had coverage through Medicare+Choice plans. CMS estimated that 10 percent of Medicare beneficiaries (approximately 4.4 million people) had no prescription drug coverage six months after Part D was implemented.[10] The share of Medicare beneficiaries without prescription drug coverage remained 10 percent in 2010, although enrollment in Part D had reached 27.7 million beneficiaries, representing 60 percent of total Medicare enrollment.[11]

On average, beneficiaries receive a federal subsidy of about three-quarters of the costs of the basic Part D benefit, and their own premium payments cover the remaining one-quarter of costs. UIS beneficiaries—about 40 percent of Part D enrollment—receive additional federal assistance that is based on their financial status. That additional benefit, which is determined on the basis of a sliding scale of income and assets, ranges from a partial subsidy of the beneficiary's Part D premium and out-of-pocket expenses to a full subsidy that covers the entire premium and all of the beneficiary's out-of-pocket expenses.

NON-LIS BENEFICIARIES

Beneficiaries who enroll in the Part D benefit but do not receive the additional low-income subsidy represent about 60 percent of all Part D beneficiaries and about 25 percent of all federal spending on Part D. Non-UIS beneficiaries account for a much smaller share of federal spending because they spend less, on average, than do UIS beneficiaries, and because they generally cover a larger share of that spending through their own premiums and out-of-pocket payments. The share of drug spending paid by non-LIS beneficiaries varies considerably across enrollees, however, depending on their total drug expenditures and the plans in which they enroll.

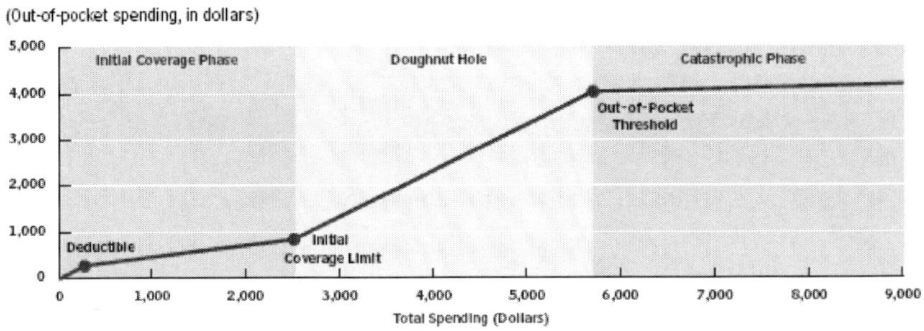

Source: Congressional Budget Office.

Note: "Total spending" refers to drug spending per beneficiary by all payers combined, including plan sponsors, beneficiaries, the federal government, and third-party payers. "Out-of-pocket spending" refers to payments made solely by beneficiaries.

Figure 1. Out-of-Pocket Spending as a Function of Total Spending Under the Standard Part D Benefit, 2008.

PART D INSURANCE PLANS AND THE STANDARD BENEFIT

In general, Medicare Part D beneficiaries are entitled to a basic benefit plan—known as a defined standard plan. That plan consists of three phases of coverage:

- The initial coverage phase, which encompasses two narrower phases of spending:

- The deductible, which is a fixed dollar amount the beneficiary must pay before the insurer begins to pay for covered pharmaceuticals.
- Expenses the beneficiary incurs after the deductible has been paid and before the initial coverage limit (ICL) has been met. Beneficiaries are responsible for 25 percent of expenditures in this range.

- The coverage gap, which includes spending between the ICL and the out-of-pocket threshold. This phase of spending is also known as the doughnut hole because, until very recently, the beneficiary was responsible for all spending in that range. The recent health care legislation changed cost sharing in this coverage phase; its implications will be discussed below.
- The catastrophic phase, which refers to spending above the out-of-pocket threshold. Once the threshold has been met, beneficiaries are responsible for 5 percent of further drug spending.

Thus, the beneficiary's out-of-pocket spending depends on total spending for that beneficiary in a complicated way (see Figure 1). The Medicare Modernization Act set the initial Part D benefit parameters and directed CMS to index them to the growth in program spending. In 2008, the deductible was $275, the ICL was $2,510, and the out-of-pocket threshold was $4,050. For those parameter values, total spending at the out-of-pocket threshold was $5,726.25. The minimum out-of-pocket cost in the catastrophic phase was $2.25 for a 30-day supply of a generic drug or preferred multisource brand drug (a brand-name drug with generic competitors that is listed on a preferred tier of a plan's formulary) and $5.60 for any other brand-name drug.[12] Provisions of the Patient Protection and Affordable Care Act (PPACA, Public Law 111-148), as amended by the Health Care and Education Reconciliation Act of 2010 (the Reconciliation Act, Public Law 111-152), changed some of the parameters of the Part D benefit, primarily those affecting the doughnut hole. Those changes and their expected effect on Part D drug use will be described below.

Part D insurance plans vary along two primary dimensions: benefit design and integration with other Medicare services. In 2008, fewer than 10 percent of non-LIS beneficiaries were enrolled in defined standard plans with the benefit design described above. One-third were enrolled in "actuarially equivalent" plans that were projected to cover the same percentage of drug expenditures. Many of those plans stipulated that, after beneficiaries had met the deductible, their out-of-pocket spending take the form of copayments (fixed-dollar amounts that depend on where the drug is placed on a plan's formulary) rather than coinsurance (a fixed percentage of the drug's price). Some of those plans offered a smaller deductible that was offset by higher cost sharing before the ICL was reached. The other 60 percent of non-LIS beneficiaries were enrolled in "enhanced" plans for which they paid a premium surcharge for supplemental benefits. Those additional benefits include some combination of the following: a reduced deductible, reduced cost sharing during the initial coverage phase, and coverage in the doughnut hole.

The degree to which stand-alone drug plans and Medicare Advantage (MA) drug plans are integrated with other Medicare services differs. Stand-alone plans are offered independently of any other insurance plan or service, whereas MA drug plans are part of broader MA plans that include medical—that is, physicians' and hospital— services. In general, beneficiaries cannot choose Medicare Advantage for medical services and a stand-alone plan for pharmaceutical services, nor can they choose FFS Medicare for medical services and Medicare Advantage for pharmaceutical services.[13] Furthermore, beneficiaries who choose to enroll in MA plans for both medical and pharmaceutical services cannot choose different plan sponsors for the two services. MA plans differ from stand-alone plans in an important way: The linkage between insuring medical and pharmaceutical expenditures in MA plans creates an incentive for those plans to manage overall expenditures rather than manage drug expenditures alone. Thus, an MA plan might offer lower cost sharing for maintenance prescriptions than for other types of prescriptions, which could reduce hospital expenditures, whereas a stand-alone plan might offer similar levels of cost sharing for both maintenance and nonmaintenance prescriptions.[14] Perhaps because of that difference, many MA plan sponsors encourage enrollment in enhanced plans by offering low premiums or by offering only an enhanced plan.[15] In MA plans, the greater beneficiary expense for the enhanced plan is often offset by average medical service costs that are below a regional benchmark, and that difference is often applied to reducing the premiums for Parts B and D. It can also be used to increase plan generosity by covering additional services or reducing cost sharing.[16]

The premium for a Part D plan depends upon the cost of the chosen plan and the national average cost for all plans. In June of each year, plan sponsors submit bids to CMS that reflect the expected per-enrollee cost of providing benefits and anticipated administrative costs (including plan profits) for a representative set of beneficiaries in the following plan year. CMS calculates a base premium from the sponsors' bids that is equal to 25.5 percent of the estimated average cost of the basic benefit; in 2008, the base premium was $27.93 per month.[17] The federal government subsidizes the remaining 74.5 percent. Plan premiums are calculated as the base premium plus the difference between that plan's bid and the national average bid. (Plans that cost less than the national average have lower premiums than the base premium.) Enhanced plan bids are separated into basic and enhanced components because the federal government does not subsidize the enhanced portion of the benefit. Premiums for enhanced plans follow this same calculation for the basic portion of the bid, and the enhanced portion of the bid is added in total to the beneficiary share of the basic premium. In 2008, the average monthly premium for Part D beneficiaries was $24.85.[18] A key reason that this average premium is below the base premium is the ability of MA plan sponsors to subsidize the premiums for their Part D plans.

DISTRIBUTION OF SPENDING AMONG NON-LIS BENEFICIARIES

In any given year, total spending on prescription drugs varies widely among beneficiaries. Total spending for over three-quarters of non-UIS beneficiaries was less than $2,510 in 2008—that is, they did not reach the doughnut hole (see Figure 2). Their total spending represented 38 percent of spending for non-UIS beneficiaries that year. Nearly one-quarter of non-UIS beneficiaries ended the year in the doughnut hole; their total spending accounted for 45 percent of spending for all non-UIS beneficiaries. Three percent of beneficiaries exceeded $4,050 in out-of-pocket expenditures and thus entered the catastrophic phase; their total spending represented 17 percent of all non-UIS spending.

Another way to categorize spending for pharmaceuticals under Part D is by the phase of coverage at the time expenses are incurred. That categorization differs from the categorization by total spending because beneficiaries who end up in the doughnut hole or catastrophic phase by the end of the year will have spent some time in earlier coverage phases. As a result, those beneficiaries will have faced different levels of cost sharing during the year.

Whereas some beneficiaries estimate their total expected drug spending for the year and make purchasing decisions accordingly, others make each purchasing decision individually and only complete the purchases that are considered worth the cost at the time. Beneficiaries with limited savings are more likely to fall in the second category, and their purchasing decisions may vary with the coverage phase. For example, while in the doughnut hole, they may attempt to stretch their supply of medication by splitting pills or by not adhering strictly to drug regimens.[19]

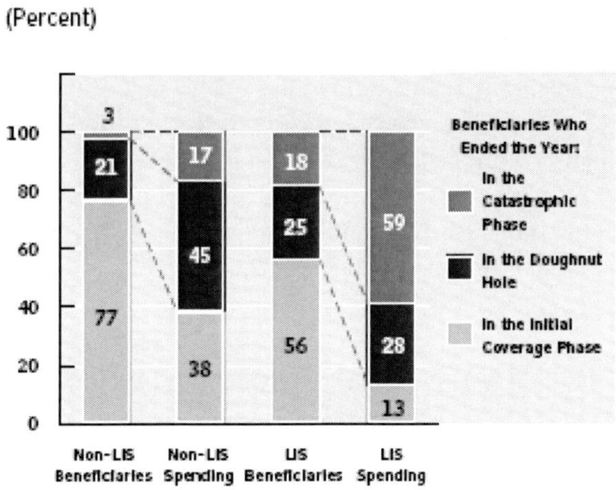

Source: Congressional Budget Office.

Notes: "Total spending" refers to drug spending per beneficiary by all payers combined, including plan sponsors, beneficiaries, the federal government, and third-party payers.

LIS = low-income subsidy.

Figure 2. Distribution of Part D Beneficiaries and Total Spending Across Coverage Phases, 2008.

Table 1. Total Spending Across Coverage Phases, by LIS Status, 2008

(Percent)		
Coverage Phase	Non-LIS	LIS
Initial	71	44
Doughnut Hole	21	28
Catastrophic	8	28

Source: Congressional Budget Office.

Notes: "Total spending" refers to drug spending per beneficiary by all payers combined, including plan sponsors, beneficiaries, the federal government, and third-party payers.

LIS = low-income subsidy.

In 2008, 71 percent of total non-UIS spending occurred while beneficiaries were in the initial coverage phase (see Table 1). That amount included all spending for beneficiaries who did not reach the doughnut hole as well as spending in the initial coverage phase for those who did reach the doughnut hole. Beneficiaries paid out of pocket for an average of 29 percent of prescription drug spending in the initial coverage phase. That out-of-pocket percentage was greater than 25 percent because many beneficiaries were responsible for 100 percent of spending until they reached their deductible.

Twenty-one percent of total non-UIS spending in 2008 occurred while beneficiaries were in the doughnut hole. Of that spending, beneficiaries paid over 60 percent out of pocket. Supplemental coverage available through enhanced plans or offered by third-party payers (such as employment-based plans, which “wrap around” the Part D benefit by covering some of beneficiaries’ out-of- pocket costs) paid for the rest of those expenditures. The remaining 8 percent of total non-UIS spending in 2008 occurred in the catastrophic phase. Comparing that statistic with the share of spending attributable to those who entered the catastrophic phase (17 percent) reveals that spending in the catastrophic phase was nearly half of total spending for those beneficiaries—indicating its importance to that group. Beneficiaries paid out of pocket for an average of 5 percent of spending in that phase, which is equal to the share that they were responsible for under the standard benefit.

Table 2. Utilization of the Part D Benefit and Average Prescription Prices, by Range of Total Spending, 2008

Total Spending (Dollars)	Percentage of Beneficiaries	Number of Prescriptions Filled Per Month[a]		Average Prescription Price (Dollars)[a, b]	Average Generic Share of Prescriptions (Percent)[c]
			Non-LIS Beneficiaries		
0	7.5	n.a.		n.a.	n.a.
0 to 500	23.1	1.5		22	83
500 to 1,500	27.4	3.2		36	70
1,500 to 2,500	18.3	4.4		49	62
2,500 to 3,500	11.8	5.2		57	58

Table 2. (Continued)

Total Spending (Dollars)	Percentage of Beneficiaries	Number of Prescriptions Filled Per Month[a]		Average Prescription Price (Dollars)[a, b]	Average Generic Share of Prescriptions (Percent)[c]
3,500 to 4,500	4.9	6.2		63	56
4,500 to 5,500	2.6	7.0		70	54
5,500 or more	4.4	8.5		135	51
			LIS Beneficiaries		
0	9.2	n.a.		n.a.	n.a.
0 to 500	15.9	1.4		24	83
500 to 1,500	17.8	3.3		40	72
1,500 to 2,500	13.2	4.5		50	65
2,500 to 3,500	10.2	5.5		59	62
3,500 to 4,500	7.7	6.4		67	59
4,500 to 5,500	5.8	7.1		74	57
5,500 or more	20.2	9.2		130	53

Source: Congressional Budget Office.

Notes: "Total spending" refers to drug spending per beneficiary by all payers combined, including plan sponsors, beneficiaries, the federal government, and third-party payers. Each range of spending includes amounts of spending from just above the lower end of the range to the upper end of the range.

LIS = low-income subsidy; n.a. = not applicable.

[a] Prescriptions with more than a 30-day supply are adjusted to equal the number and average price of a 30-day supply. Prescriptions with less than a 30-day supply are counted as a single prescription.

[b] Prescription prices include sales tax and dispensing fees paid to the pharmacy.

[c] Generic drugs are identified using the Medicaid classification system.

DRIVERS OF HIGHER SPENDING AMONG NON-LIS BENEFICIARIES

Greater prescription drug spending is driven by two factors: the filling of a larger number of prescriptions and the filling of prescriptions for more-expensive drugs.

Both factors played a role in higher total spending per non-UIS beneficiary in 2008, but the number of prescriptions seems to have been a greater driver of higher expenditures than was the average price of a prescription. For example, compared with non-UIS beneficiaries for whom total spending was between zero and $500, those with total spending between $4,500 and $5,500 filled nearly five times the number of prescriptions per month (see Table 2). The average prescription price in that category of spending was about three times more than the average price of a prescription filled by people with total spending between zero and $500.

The average prescription price was substantially greater in the group with spending above $5,500 than in all other groups, probably because beneficiaries with the highest spending are, in general, more likely to suffer from chronic conditions (such as multiple sclerosis and rheumatoid arthritis) that require ongoing treatment with specialty drugs (such as biologics).[20] Those types of drugs are typically very expensive.[21] One study found that 31 percent of beneficiaries without the low-income subsidy who used at least one specialty drug reached the out-of-pocket threshold.[22] Given that only 3 percent of non-LIS beneficiaries reached the out-of-pocket threshold, that finding implies that those who used specialty drugs were at least 10 times as likely to reach the out-of-pocket threshold as those who did not use specialty drugs.

The relationship between spending and the use of generic drugs is also noteworthy. Generics, which often are much less expensive than their brand-name counterparts, made up a smaller share of prescriptions for beneficiaries with greater total drug expenditures. On average, the retail price of a generic drug is 25 percent of the retail price of a brand-name drug of the same chemical makeup.[23] Thus, choosing brands over their generic counterparts could have played a role in higher spending. However, CBO recently found that the generic utilization rate among Part D beneficiaries was over 90 percent in 2007 when a generic option was available.[24] That statistic suggests that while brand usage was sometimes a matter of preference, it often reflected the lack of availability of equivalent generics. Although there may be additional room for switching to a generic alternative within the same therapeutic class when no direct generic substitute is available, such switches might not always be clinically indicated. Newer brand-name drugs tend to be more expensive and are less likely to face generic competition, and that is especially true for specialty drugs.

THE FEDERAL CONTRIBUTION TO PART D SPENDING FOR NON-LIS BENEFICIARIES

In 2008, the federal government paid for approximately 40 percent of total Part D spending for non-LIS beneficiaries. Premiums are set so that the federal government pays for 74.5 percent of the basic benefit, which itself covered 53 percent of spending by non-LIS enrollees. Applying the federal government's share of the basic benefit to that percentage provides a rough estimate of the federal share of non-LIS spending.[25] Nearly 85 percent of federal spending for the basic benefit funded the initial coverage phase portion of the benefit; the remainder funded the catastrophic portion.

Most of the remaining 60 percent of total Part D spending for non-LIS beneficiaries was paid by the beneficiaries through out-of-pocket spending and premium payments (which covered the beneficiary's share of the basic benefit and any enhanced coverage). Less than 2 percent of spending was covered by third-party payers, such as state pharmaceutical assistance programs and workers' compensation programs.

IMPLICATIONS OF RECENT HEALTH CARE LEGISLATION FOR NON-LIS BENEFICIARIES

Various provisions of PPACA and the Reconciliation Act have a sizable impact on the Part D benefit for non-LIS enrollees.[26] Those new laws change the Part D program in two main ways. First, the prescription drug benefit gradually becomes much more generous over the next decade, primarily by reducing beneficiaries' payments in the doughnut hole. Starting in January 2011, manufacturers of brand-name drugs began covering 50 percent of the cost of such medications for beneficiaries in the doughnut hole.[27] The standard Part D benefit will gradually fill in the rest of the doughnut hole for both brand-name and generic drugs so that, by 2020, beneficiaries' cost sharing will be reduced to 25 percent of their drug spending between the initial coverage level and the out-of-pocket threshold.[28] At that point, plans will be required to cover 75 percent of generic drug expenditures and 25 percent of brand-name drug expenditures incurred while beneficiaries are in the doughnut hole; another 50 percent of brand-name drug expenditures incurred in the doughnut hole will continue to be covered by manufacturers.[29] The additional generosity of the Part D benefit will increase the cost of the benefit in two ways: plan payments will increase for drugs purchased in the doughnut hole, and beneficiary utilization will increase because of lower out-of-pocket costs for drugs purchased in the doughnut hole.[30] Altogether, that additional generosity will raise beneficiaries' premiums by about 10 percent in 2019 relative to what would have occurred otherwise.[31]

The drug benefit will also become more generous because the out-of-pocket threshold will increase more slowly than will the other benefit parameters from 2014 through 2020, after which the threshold will return to what it would have been if its growth rate had not been slowed.[32] That change will reduce the amount of money a beneficiary must spend before reaching the out-of-pocket threshold and entering the catastrophic phase. If the benefit parameters described in this section for the year 2020 had been applied to drug purchases in 2008, beneficiaries who ended the year in the doughnut hole and catastrophic phase would have saved an average of $550 and $2,150 in out-of-pocket expenditures, respectively.[33]

The second change to the Part D program was to introduce income-based premiums (which are also used in Medicare Part B) for individuals with income above $85,000 and couples with a joint income above $170,000, beginning in 2011. The additional premium ranges from $12 per month for those whose income is just above the thresholds to nearly $70 per month for individuals with income exceeding $214,000 or couples with a joint income exceeding $428,000.[34] Approximately 5 percent of beneficiaries will pay a higher premium because of this policy change. Some Part D beneficiaries may drop coverage, and future Medicare enrollees may forgo enrollment in Part D, because of the premium increase. However, because the premium remains heavily subsidized for most people, the income-based premium is unlikely to change enrollment decisions for most of the affected beneficiaries.

LIS Beneficiaries

In addition to the standard Part D benefit offered to all Medicare beneficiaries, the federal government provides an additional benefit—the low-income subsidy—to some beneficiaries. Eligibility for the low-income subsidy and the generosity of the subsidy depend on the beneficiary's income and assets. The most generous LIS benefit covers all premium payments and out-of-pocket expenses for beneficiaries enrolled in both Medicare and Medicaid— known as dual-eligibles—who reside in a long-term care facility. The least generous LIS benefit covers a small share of the Part D premium and subsidizes beneficiaries' out-of-pocket spending so that they pay 15 percent of total costs until they reach the catastrophic phase. Once those beneficiaries enter the catastrophic phase, they pay 5 percent of prescription costs, the same rate paid by enrollees without the low-income subsidy.[35] That benefit level applies to beneficiaries with income between 135 percent and 150 percent of the federal poverty level who are not enrolled in Medicaid and whose assets are below a given threshold.[36] The generosity of the LIS benefit ranges between those two benefit levels for the remaining LIS population, although most of the variation is in the degree of cost sharing: 98 percent of LIS beneficiaries received the full premium subsidy in 2008.[37] Because of those additional subsidies, the differences among plan types experienced by the non-LIS population are greatly muted for the LIS population.

Whereas many LIS enrollees were automatically enrolled in the LIS program, others actively applied for LIS enrollment. Automatic enrollees include dual-eligibles and Medicare beneficiaries who are already enrolled in a Medicare Savings Program or in Social Security's Supplemental Security Income program.[38] Because these individuals have previously met certain state income and asset tests, CMS automatically enrolls them in a Part D plan with a premium below their region's benchmark for the LIS program. (The benchmarks are based on averages of premiums for basic plans in the region, weighted by LIS enrollment per plan.) Other Medicare beneficiaries who apply for the LIS benefit must show that they meet the program's income and asset tests.[39] CMS randomly assigns those LIS beneficiaries to a benchmark Part D plan if they do not choose one. In 2008, 7.9 million beneficiaries were automatically enrolled in the LIS program, and 1.5 million were enrolled after applying.[40]

Beneficiaries for whom CMS chooses plans may switch plans if, for example, they prefer the formulary of covered drugs under another plan. However, if the chosen plan's premium is greater than the LIS benchmark premium, the beneficiary is responsible for paying the difference. Evidence suggests that LIS beneficiaries are unlikely to opt out of the plans in which they have been enrolled by CMS.[41] The LIS benefit does not pay for the additional premiums charged by enhanced plans. However, LIS benefits are more generous than enhanced benefits, and filled more-expensive prescriptions. The number of prescriptions and the average price per prescription were similar for both groups of beneficiaries within each range of spending (see Table 2 on page 6). However, LIS beneficiaries were more likely to fall into the higher-spending ranges. For instance, total spending was greater than $5,500 for 20 percent of LIS beneficiaries, whereas only 4 percent of non-LIS beneficiaries had total spending greater than that amount.

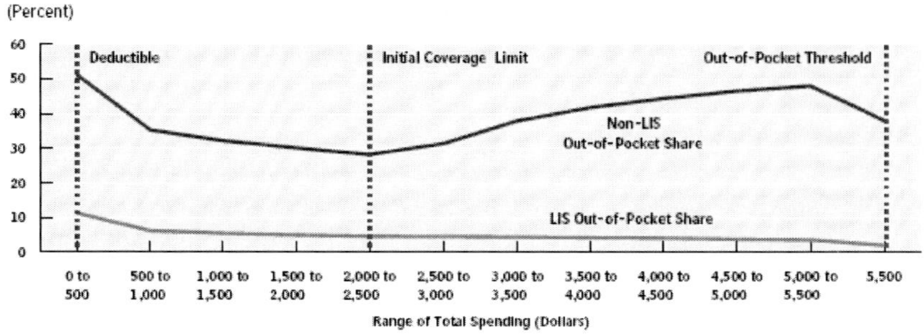

Source: Congressional Budget Office.

Notes: "Total spending" refers to drug spending per beneficiary by all payers combined, including plan sponsors, beneficiaries, the federal government, and third-party payers. "Out-of-pocket spending" refers to payments made solely by beneficiaries. Each range of spending includes amounts of spending from just above the lower end of the range to the upper end of the range.

The vertical lines indicate the spending range in which each labeled point in the benefit design occurs. LIS = low-income subsidy.

Figure 3. Out-of-Pocket Spending as a Share of Total Spending, by LIS Status, 2008.

THE FEDERAL CONTRIBUTION TO SPENDING FOR LIS BENEFICIARIES

The federal government paid for approximately 95 percent of Part D prescription drug spending for LIS beneficiaries in 2008.[42] That large share is attributable to two features of the Part D program: First, the federal government pays for nearly all of LIS beneficiaries' premiums for the basic benefit, which covered 56 percent of spending for LIS enrollees in 2008. Second, the federal government subsidizes most of LIS beneficiaries' out-of-pocket spending, which represented 40 percent of LIS expenditures. Overall, 43 percent of federal spending for LIS beneficiaries funded expenditures in the initial coverage phase, and the remaining federal spending was split between the doughnut hole and the catastrophic phase.

COMPARING NON-LIS AND LIS BENEFICIARIES

Beneficiaries who receive the low-income subsidy in Medicare Part D differ in various ways from those who do not. To begin with, the relationship between total Part D spending and out-of-pocket spending is quite different for the two populations. Among non-LIS beneficiaries in 2008, out-of-pocket spending as a share of total spending varied greatly across spending levels (see Figure 3). Beneficiaries with low total spending paid a large share out of pocket because the deductible accounted for most of their spending. The out-of-pocket share was smaller for beneficiaries with greater total spending—up to the ICL—because the deductible represented a smaller share of total spending. The out-of-pocket share rose for beneficiaries for whom total spending exceeded the ICL because spending in the doughnut hole was largely out of pocket. Beneficiaries who surpassed the out-of-pocket threshold paid for a smaller share of their total spending, although they spent a substantial amount to reach the catastrophic phase. In 2008, average out-of-pocket spending among non-LIS beneficiaries who reached the catastrophic phase was $4,000.

LIS beneficiaries do not experience the same variation in their out-of-pocket share of spending. Their out-of-pocket share is much lower than that of non-LIS beneficiaries and mostly flat across total spending levels. Among LIS beneficiaries in 2008, there was a slight negative relationship between total spending and the out-of-pocket share of that spending. That pattern probably arose because LIS beneficiaries with higher expenditures were more likely to be enrolled in a more generous category of the LIS benefit, in which a greater share of out-of-pocket expenditures was subsidized.

Another significant difference between the two categories of enrollees lies in the distribution of beneficiaries across spending levels. LIS beneficiaries are much more likely than non-LIS beneficiaries to fall into higher-spending categories and less likely to fall into lower-spending categories (see Figure 4). For example, only 24 percent of non-LIS beneficiaries exceeded $2,500 in total spending in 2008, but 44 percent of LIS beneficiaries exceeded that spending level (see Table 3). Similarly, only 6 percent of non-LIS beneficiaries exceeded $5,000 in total spending, whereas 23 percent of LIS beneficiaries exceeded that amount.

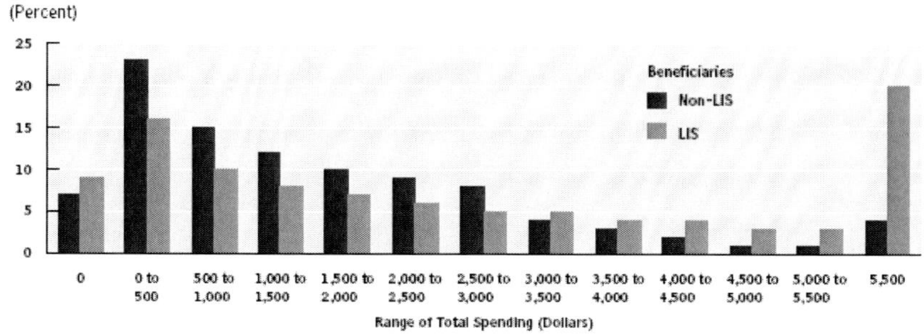

Source: Congressional Budget Office.

Notes: "Total spending" refers to drug spending per beneficiary by all payers combined, including plan sponsors, beneficiaries, the federal government, and third-party payers. Each range of spending includes amounts of spending from just above the lower end of the range to equal to the upper end of the range.

LIS = low-income subsidy.

Figure 4. Distribution of Part D Beneficiaries Across Ranges of Total Spending, by LIS Status, 2008.

Yet another distinction between the two groups of enrollees is that LIS beneficiaries constituted 40 percent of Part D enrollment in 2008 but accounted for 55 percent of total prescription drug expenditures that year. At $3,600, the average per capita expenditures for those beneficiaries were twice as large as the expenditures for their counterparts ($1,800). That difference is probably partly attributable to the difference in generosity of the two benefits. The out-of-pocket share of spending is much lower for LIS beneficiaries than for non-LIS beneficiaries. In addition, many LIS beneficiaries pay the same amount out of pocket for all brand-name drugs, regardless of the drugs' price or whether the drugs have preferred status. Moreover, MedPAC found that generic dispensing rates were lower for LIS beneficiaries for several therapeutic classes.[43]

Average spending in the two groups also differs in part because LIS beneficiaries tend to be sicker than non-LIS beneficiaries. That tendency is suggested by three types of statistics: the original reason for Medicare eligibility; risk scores; and the presence of chronic disease. CBO found that, in 2008, 85 percent of non-LIS beneficiaries became eligible for Medicare because they turned 65, and the remaining 15 percent became eligible before turning 65 by successfully applying for the Social Security Disability Insurance (SSDI) program.[44] By contrast, half of LIS beneficiaries became eligible for Medicare by qualifying for SSDI, suggesting that a larger share of that group had poorer health status.

Table 3. Shares of Part D Beneficiaries and Spending in Two Higher Ranges of Total Spending, 2008

(Percent)

	Greater Than $2,500	Greater Than $5,000
Non-UIS		
Beneficiaries	24	6
Spending	62	28
UIS		
Beneficiaries	44	23
Spending	87	66

Source: Congressional Budget Office.

Notes: "Total spending" refers to drug spending per beneficiary by all payers combined, including plan sponsors, beneficiaries, the federal government, and third-party payers.

LIS = low-income subsidy.

Further, in calculating payments to Part D plans, CMS develops risk scores to ensure that plans are compensated for enrolling sicker beneficiaries. Those risk scores reflect differences in medical disabilities, previous diagnoses, and demographics, and they are designed to predict differences in expected drug utilization. In 2008, risk scores indicated that LIS beneficiaries would probably have 15 percent greater drug expenditures than non-LIS beneficiaries.[45] Moreover, research has shown that the risk-adjustment methodology being used in 2008 overpredicted costs for low-spending enrollees and under-predicted costs for high-spending enrollees, which has led CMS to update its risk-adjustment methodology more recently.[46]

Lastly, LIS beneficiaries have a higher prevalence of chronic conditions and comorbidities (additional diseases and conditions) than do non-LIS beneficiaries. One study on the prevalence of chronic conditions among dual-eligibles (two-thirds of the LIS population) found that 63 percent of dual-eligibles had multiple chronic physical conditions. By contrast, 53 percent of other Medicare beneficiaries fell into that category.[47] More strikingly, 20 percent of dual-eligibles had multiple mental or cognitive conditions; only 5 percent of other Medicare beneficiaries did so. Some of those conditions, such as depression and schizophrenia, require very expensive drug regimens. Likewise, 38 percent of dual-eligibles had both a mental or cognitive condition and a chronic physical condition compared with 17 percent of other Medicare beneficiaries. Differences in the prevalence of chronic conditions among the two populations are strong indicators of differences in the need for medical and pharmaceutical services.

End Notes

[1] Title I of Public Law 108-173, 117 Stat. 2066, 2071–2176.

[2] Department of Health and Human Services, Centers for Medicare and Medicaid Services, Office of the Actuary, 2011 Annual Report of the Boards of Trustees of the Federal Hospital Insurance and Federal Supplementary Medical Insurance Trust Funds (May 2011).

[3] In addition, the Medicare Modernization Act created a subsidy for firms that offer outpatient prescription drug coverage for their retirees. The population that receives assistance through the retiree drug subsidy is excluded from this analysis.

[4] That spending takes various forms: Plan sponsors' payments are financed by enrollees' premium payments and federal premium subsidies. Beneficiaries' out-of-pocket spending (beyond the premium payments to plan sponsors) consists of deductibles, coinsurance, and copayments. The federal government's spending (beyond the premium subsidies paid to plan sponsors) consists of cost-sharing subsidies. Third-party payers are entities other than a beneficiary (first party) or insurance plans (second party) that finance pharmaceutical spending.

[5] Unless otherwise specified, all statistics stem from CBO's analysis of Part D claims data for calendar year 2008 and associated data files that describe beneficiary characteristics (such as demographic information).

[6] Medicare Part B provided limited coverage of self-administered drugs, generally for the treatment of cancer and posttransplant immunosuppression.

[7] Congressional Budget Office, Issues in Designing a Prescription Drug Benefit for Medicare (October 2002).

[8] People who are eligible for Medicare but have another source of creditable coverage for pharmaceuticals, such as employment-based coverage, are exempt from the late-enrollment penalty. In 2008, CMS defined "creditable coverage" as benefits that covered at least 60 percent of an enrollee's drug costs, on average, and that satisfied certain access and minimum benefit requirements.

[9] Kaiser Family Foundation, "Medicare: The Medicare Prescription Drug Benefit," Kaiser Family Foundation Fact Sheet (November 2006).

[10] Ibid.

[11] Kaiser Family Foundation, "Medicare: The Medicare Prescription Drug Benefit," Kaiser Family Foundation Fact Sheet (October 2010).

[12] In 2011, the deductible is $310, the initial coverage limit is $2,840, and the out-of-pocket threshold is $4,550. The minimum out-of-pocket costs in the catastrophic phase are $2.50 for a 30-day supply of a generic or preferred multisource brand prescription and $6.30 for a brand-name prescription.

[13] Some MA plans do not offer a corresponding prescription drug plan (referred to as an MA-PD); in those cases, enrollees may choose a stand-alone drug plan for their Part D benefit.

[14] Maintenance drugs are prescribed for chronic conditions that require ongoing treatment.

[15] See Medicare Payment Advisory Commission (MedPAC), Report to the Congress: Medicare Payment Policy (March 2011), p. 323.

[16] See MedPAC, Medicare Advantage Program Payment System (October 2010).

[17] See MedPAC, Report to the Congress (March 2011), p. 332.

[18] See MedPAC, Report to the Congress: Medicare Payment Policy (March 2009), p. 290.

[19]. MedPAC, Experiences Obtaining Drugs Under Part D: Focus Groups with Beneficiaries, Physicians, and Pharmacists, No. 08-4 (prepared by National Opinion Research Center, May 2008).

[20] Biologics are derived from living organisms and generally are more complex and more expensive to produce than chemically based drugs.

[21] CMS allows Part D plans to label drugs as specialty drugs if the monthly cost of those medications exceeds a set threshold. That threshold was $600 in 2008.

[22] Government Accountability Office, Medicare Part D: Spending, Beneficiary Cost Sharing, and Cost-Containment Efforts for High-Cost Drugs Eligible for a Specialty Tier, GAO-10-242 (January 29, 2010).

[23] Congressional Budget Office, Effects of Using Generic Drugs on Medicare's Prescription Drug Spending (September 2010).

[24] Ibid.

[25] Because total spending is lower for non-LIS beneficiaries, that population accounts for a smaller share of total spending for the basic benefit than the LIS population. Since the 74.5 percent average is applied to total basic benefit spending, the federal government covers a slightly smaller share of basic benefit spending (69 percent) for the non-LIS population.

[26] P.L. 111-148, 124 Stat. 119, and P.L. 111-152, 124 Stat. 1029, respectively.

[27] Section 3301 of PPACA.

[28] Section 1101 of the Reconciliation Act.

[29] Section 3301 of PPACA.

[30] In addition, CBO expects that the various provisions of PPACA and the Reconciliation Act will push up the prices of certain prescription drugs and thereby make federal costs for the Part D benefit slightly higher. See Congressional Budget Office, letter to the Honorable Paul Ryan about the effects on prescription drug prices of certain provisions of the Patient Protection and Affordable Care Act and the Health Care and Education Reconciliation Act of 2010 (November 4, 2010).

[31] For more information, see Congressional Budget Office, "Comparison of Projected Medicare Part D Premiums Under Current Law and Under Reconciliation Legislation Combined with H.R. 3590 as Passed by the Senate" (March 19, 2010).

[32] From 2014 to 2015, the growth rate of the out-of-pocket threshold will be 0.25 percentage points below the growth rate of Part D expenses. From 2016 to 2019, the out-of-pocket threshold will be indexed to the consumer price index for all urban consumers plus 2 percentage points, which will most likely be lower than the growth of Part D expenses. See section 1101 of the Reconciliation Act.

[33] This calculation does not account for any increase in prescription drug spending that would have resulted from reduced out-of-pocket spending.

[34] Married beneficiaries who file separately reach this maximum additional payment when their individual income is greater than $129,000.

[35] The cost-sharing subsidy counts as out-of-pocket spending; thus, LIS beneficiaries reach the out-of-pocket threshold at the same level of total spending as non-LIS beneficiaries in their same plan.

[36] In 2008, the federal poverty level was $10,400 for a single person and $14,000 for a couple. The asset threshold was $11,990 for a single person and $23,970 for a couple.

[37] Department of Health and Human Services, 2011 Annual Report of the Boards of Trustees of the Federal Hospital Insurance and Federal Supplementary Medical Insurance Trust Funds.

[38] Medicare Savings Programs are administered by Medicaid; they are designed to help Medicare beneficiaries who have limited income and few other resources pay for their premiums and cost sharing for Parts A and B of Medicare.

[39] Kaiser Family Foundation, "Medicare: The Medicare Prescription Drug Benefit," Kaiser Family Foundation Fact Sheet (February 2008).

[40] Ibid.

[41] Research has shown that LIS beneficiaries were unlikely to choose a new plan after CMS reassigned them to a new Part D plan because their previously assigned plan no longer held benchmark status. See Grecia Marrufo and others, Evaluation of the Medicare Demonstration to Transition Enrollment of Low Income Subsidy Beneficiaries (report submitted by Acumen, LLC, to the Centers for Medicare and Medicaid Services, June 2009).

[42]. Because the Medicaid program paid for pharmaceutical expenditures for dual-eligibles before Part D was implemented, a provision of the Medicare Modernization Act requires states to reimburse the federal government for a portion of those expenditures. Those reimbursements are included in CBO's estimates of federal Part D spending.

[43]. Shinobu Suzuki, "MedPAC Analysis of Factors Affecting LIS Use of Prescription Drugs" (presented at the Centers for Medicare and Medicaid Services Part D Data Symposium, Baltimore, Md., March 18, 2010).

[44] Individuals with end-stage renal disease are also eligible for Medicare within three months of their first dialysis treatment.

[45] Beneficiaries without the low-income subsidy had an average risk score of 1.025, and LIS beneficiaries had an average risk score of 1.181. To reflect the fact that the risk adjustment methodology imperfectly predicts utilization for those populations, CMS further adjusts these risk scores for beneficiaries who have the LIS benefit or are institutionalized. See MedPAC, A Data Book: Health Care Spending and the Medicare Program (June 2010).

[46] John Hsu and others, "Distributing $800 Billion: An Early Assessment of Medicare Part D Risk Adjustment," Health Affairs, vol. 28, no. 1 (January 2009), pp. 215–225.

[47] Judy Kasper, Molly O'Malley Watts, and Barbara Lyons, Chronic Disease and Co-Morbidity Among Dual Eligibles: Implications for Patterns of Medicaid and Medicare Service Use and Spending, Kaiser Commission on Medicaid and the Uninsured, Issue Paper No. 8081 (July 2010).

INDEX

D

E

F

G

S

T

U

V

W

Y